PRAISE FOR RAISING LITTLE KIDS WITH BIG LOVE

These are excellent books. The *1 Corinthians 13 Parent* series has a great idea. It takes a new spin on a common passage and applies it to the family. It's fresh. It's new but it's based in the scriptures. People will love the idea. This is a winner in my opinion.

-Dr. Scott Turansky, National Center for Biblical Parenting and author

In *Raising Little Kids with Big Love,* parenting experts, Lori Wildenberg and Becky Danielson give practical insight to how we can love our children well and what that looks like in real life. Using 1 Corinthians 13 as the foundation, *Raising Little Kids with a Big Love* weaves together parenting stories with solutions from Scripture that are sure to give parents the tools they need to demonstrate big love on a daily basis. I highly recommend this book for parents with children of all ages and for small group or individual study as well.

-Stephanie Shott, founder of The M.O.M. Initiative and author of *The Making of a Mom*

Lori and Becky effectively blend scriptural principles and real life examples into both books in the *1 Corinthians 13 Parent* Series. Each page is a mirror that will reflect the reader's parenting strengths and challenges. Parents, be encouraged...you are not alone. You will be helped in this invaluable calling. I highly recommend the *1 Corinthians 13* Parent series books to anyone looking to evaluate, tweak, or implement a spiritually-based parenting plan.

-Kirk Weaver, Family Time Training Founder and Executive Director

Clear the bookshelves parents, *Raising Little Kids with Big Love* has solid biblical foundation to break the cycle of parent-child struggles. Each chapter contributes to your parenting style and the needs of your unique child. Lori and Becky invite you to walk through fifteen transforming principles based on 1 Corinthians 13:4-8, which will not only help you become a better parent, but will also help build relationships with your children that will last a lifetime. This book is a must have arsenal for every parent.

-Heather Riggleman, blogger at heatherriggleman.com and author of *Mama Needs a Time Out*

In *Raising Little Kids with Big Love*, Lori Wildenberg and Becky Danielson display not only a heart for children, but an insightful passion to help parents consider the primary place of influence they hold in the development and formation of their kids. Throughout the book, the authors highlight key points of learning and offer key questions, as well as suggestions intended to give parents the right tools to raise their children to love, honor, and respect both God and others. The book serves as a reminder that God is Love and that parents have the awesome privilege and responsibility to reflect that love to their children. The authors remind us that parenting is a holy calling and not to be taken for granted. Read, reflect, and learn!

-Reverend Mark R. Stromberg, Superintendent of the Northwest Conference of the Evangelical Covenant Church of America

The 1 *Corinthians 13 Parent* Series has fresh ideas and great reminders on parenting kids of all ages and stages. Becky and Lori ask great questions to help you identify your current style of parenting. They also provide biblical support to try new techniques. These books are powerful resources you will want to use for years to come.

-Peter J. Larson, Ph.D., psychologist, President of Life Innovations, co-author of *Prepare/Enrich Couple Checkup Assessment Tools* and *10 Great Dates to Grow Together Spiritually* (co-authored with Heather Larson, David and Claudia Arp)

-Heather Larson, M.A., Associate Director of Marriage Alive, co-author of *10 Great Dates to Grow Together Spiritually* (co-authors Peter Larson, David and Claudia Arp)

In a world where parenting often seems overwhelming, Becky Danielson and Lori Wildenberg deliver an approach to parenting little kids that's so simple that it's brilliant. With a style that's based on the unfailing love of Christ, the authors guide parents with simple tips, compelling stories, and the motivation to make it through those tough days with biblical concepts and a huge dose of hope. This is a must read for any parent who wants to be more Christlike in her attitudes and in doing so, raise kids who learn to love Jesus with a big love.

-Erin MacPherson, author of *The Christian Mama's Guide* series.

We moms know we're supposed to love our kids, but what does that look like in day-to-day parenting? In *Raising Little Kids with Big Love*, Lori and Becky show us exactly that! By exploring each quality of love in 1 Corinthians 13 and relating it to mothering, Lori and Becky teach us how to do what we want most to do as moms—love our children well. The workbook contains thoughtful, practical questions to help us make this kind of love a reality in our family's life. This book is practical, helpful, and guaranteed to make a difference in the life of any mom who reads it!

-Megan Breedlove, author of *Chaotic Joy: Finding Abundance in the Messiness of Motherhood*

I love the concept of approaching parenting according to the attributes of love described in 1 Corinthians 13, and I love even more Lori Wildenberg's and Becky Danielson's reminder that we as parents need to practice these attributes too! In *Raising Little Kids with Big Love*, Lori and Becky are balanced, relatable, and, most of all, wise guides through just about every parenting issue I can think of. A practical and God-centered resource.

-Julia Roller, author of *Mom Seeks God*

Looking for a parenting book? Look no further! *Raising Little Kids with Big Love* provides insight and wisdom into both parent and child. "To the point" chapters target everything from meal time to bed time tips. Scriptures and prayers to pray over your child make this a must have for every mom.

-Debbie Taylor Williams, Author, Bible Teacher, Speaker
The Plan A MOM in a Plan B World, ww.debbietaylorwilliams.com

The *1 Corinthians 13 Parent: Raising Little Kids with Big Love* by Lori Wildenberg and Becky Danielson is a must-read for Christian parents. In each chapter, Lori and Becky provide tips to help parents live out the characteristics of love described in 1 Corinthians 13. The authors close each chapter with questions for deeper reflection, practical parenting tips, and a prayer. As a busy mother of two, I am thankful I took time to read this very practical book. It armed me with tools to help my days go smoother and challenged me to show my love to my children in more effective ways.

-Lindsey Bell, Author of *Searching for Sanity: 52 Insights from the Parents of the Bible* and Stay-at-Home Mother of Two

In a time when parents have a tendency to feel inadequate and believe they are just hanging on, both books in The *1 Corinthians 13 Parent* series is a breath of fresh air. The *1 Corinthians 13 Parent* books give us powerful principles, real-life examples, and a clear path to success. Not just books to read, but to study and let them take you on a journey that will make you a better parent and a better person. Every church should use these resources for small group study for parents of children of all ages.

-Dr. Chuck Stecker, President of A Chosen
Generation, Author, Speaker and Ministry

Raising a healthy, socially well-adjusted, and faith-filled adult is the goal of every Christian parent. The 1 Corinthians 13 Parent: Raising Little Kids with Big Love book is a guidebook for parenting with love and limits. Real life examples help us understand what kind of parent we are and how we may become even better. The series is a valuable, hands-on tool for raising our children. It can be used in a group or in your own family.

-Barbara Z. Carlson, coauthor of *Putting Family First: Successful Strategies for Reclaiming Family Life in a Hurry-Up World*

Parenting isn't easy! I remember days I wanted to run away. The *1 Corinthians 13 Parent: Raising Little Kids with Big Love* honestly addresses the challenges parents face without laying guilt trips. Lori and Becky have dug deeply into God's Word to provide practical advice, fresh insights, and much-needed encouragement. Highly recommended.

-Marlene Bagnull, author, conference director, mom, grandmom

The 1 CORINTHIANS 13 PARENT

Raising Little Kids with BIG Love

THE 1 CORINTHIANS 13 PARENT

RAISING LITTLE KIDS WITH BIG LOVE

LORI WILDENBERG

BECKY DANIELSON M.ED.

Bold Vision Books
PO Box 2011
Friendswood, Texas 77549

Copyright: Lori Wildenberg and Becky Danielson, 2014

ISBN #978-0-9912842-4-5

Library of Congress Control Number: LCCN 2014941306

Published in association with Books & Such Literary Management, 52 Mission Circle, Suite 122, PMB 170, Santa Rosa, CA 95409-5370 www. booksandsuch.com

Printed in the United States of America.

Cover and Interior Design by kae Creative Solutions

Editing, Deb Strubel, Katie McDivitt

Cover photograph by Michael Schneidmiller

Bold Vision Books
PO Box 2011
Friendswood, Texas 77549

DEDICATION

We dedicate *Raising Little Kids with Big Love* to our parents.

Bob and Pat Appel,
You laid the foundation for my faith.
You have shown me the value of strong family ties.
You shared your passion for prose and poetry with me.
Your love, encouragement, and support are forever
imprinted on my heart.
I love you.
-LORI
(Miss you, Pops)

Dale and Carole Erickson,
Thank you for leading me to Jesus in words
but more importantly, deeds.
xo BECKY

Love is patient,
love is kind.
It does not envy,
it does not boast,
it is not proud.

It is not rude,
it is not self-seeking,
it is not easily angered,
it keeps no record of wrongs.

Love does not delight in evil
but rejoices with the truth.
It always protects,
always trusts,
always hopes,
always perseveres.

Love never fails.

1 Corinthians 13:4–8a

CONTENTS

FOREWORD

In the name of love … read this book

I am the mom of six children. Three through birth and three through adoption. Three are adults and three are six years and under. What was I thinking? Sometimes I ask myself that.

When John and I were going through training to adopt from the foster care system I listened and (sort of) took it in. To tell you the truth I was a little bit prideful in my parenting. Yes, raising kids was hard, but I'd been a mom for 20+ years… I knew what came with the territory. (Or so I thought!)

God must have been chuckling when He gave us our three adoptive kids. They are busy, loud, and naughty. They are lovers and fighters. They bring me to my knees hourly. And once I had little ones in my home again, I remembered how really hard parenting little kids really was. I remembered the tears (mine) and the frustration (also mine). I must have blocked it all out.

Being a mom is hard. Raising little kids with big love is really hard! That's why I'm so thankful for Lori Wildenberg and Becky Danielson. They're moms and encouragers of moms. They understand.

So many times I'd pick up this manuscript when my nerves were frazzled and I was at the end of my rope. Through their words of understanding and direction I found encouragement and help.

Lori and Becky didn't write this book as two moms who have it all together (who ever does)? Instead, they write as two trusted friends. "I know how you feel. I've felt that way too. I understand, and…here's something that might help." Their advice isn't just of their own making, though. Instead, they point to the source of all wisdom, the Bible, and they show us how God's Truth can be applied to everyday parenting. More specifically, they point to 1 Corinthians 13 as a guideline of sorts. Because isn't that our role as a parent—to show love in numerous (and unnatural to our human flesh) ways?

So if you're a parent…you need this book. And if you don't have time to read because the demands on your life are so pressing, you especially need this book! Parenting is not easy, but it does get easier when you have trusted friends like Lori and Becky to point you in the right direction.

Within these pages you aren't going to find fluff or sweet words alone. Those type of books may inspire us for a few hours (or minutes) but only go so far. Instead, Lori and Becky offer real, practical advice for everyday parenting. So sit down on that curb while you watch your kid ride his trike around your driveway again and again, and take a deeper look at yourself, your kids, and God's Word with Lori and Becky's help. It's there you'll discover parenting gems that are guaranteed to help tomorrow run a little smoother than today…all in the name of love.

TRICIA GOYER
USA-Today Bestselling author of 42 books,
including *Lead Your Family Like Jesus*

Acknowledgments

First we want to express our appreciation to our agent, Mary G. Keeley of Books and Such Literary Agency. A great big thank you for believing in us and in the importance of the *1 Corinthians 13 Parent* series.

With grateful hearts we want to thank our many class participants, readers, and prayer warriors. Your contribution to this project has been invaluable.

Thank you to the following individuals for your part in bringing this project to fruition: Julianne Adams, Marlene Bagnull, Maureen Behrens, Paul and Kym Benfield, Ed and Nancy Bock, Chuck Bolton, Keri Buisman, Tim and Suanne Deskin, Jeannie Edwards, Ken and Kerry Ekstrom, Lori Hayda Felton, Jill Gillis, Tom and Lynn Halloran, Karen Hoops, Mary Heathman, Katie McElroy, Jim and Laurie Muehlbauer, Liz Manning, Karen Murkowski, Kathy Namura, Jerry and Kyndall Nixon, Carol Olsen, Amy Raye, Danielle Reeves, Melonie Richards, Darcy Roberson, Dwight and Lindee Sebald, Sara Silburn, Megan Stone, Chris and Ann Tillotson, Scott Turansky, Stacey Van Horn, Sheila Wilson, Chris and Kathy Wolfe, Stephen and Elsa Wolff, George and Cindy Wood.

Bible Study Fellowship has played a tremendous role in each of our spiritual lives. We thank God for Bev Coniaris (MN) and Tina Cotton (CO) for their faithful service and excellent teaching. You have stretched us heart, mind, and soul.

To our church families: Christ Presbyterian Church and WaterStone Community Church. With special thanks to John Crosby, Lynda English, Nick Lillo, James Madsen, Sarah Norton, and Larry Renoe.

We are blessed and honored to be ministry partners with: A Chosen Generation and National Center for Biblical Parenting. And of course those ministries represented on our 1C13P team: 10 Great Dates (David & Claudia Arp, Peter & Heather Larson), A Father's Walk (Matt Haviland),

Family Fest Ministries (Pete Larson), Family Time Training (Kirk Weaver and Jenna Hallock), The Mom Café (Chris Carter), The Single Mom (Misty Honnold), Stone Foundations of Learning, Inc. (Megan Stone), and Tonja's Table (Tonja Engen). We want to be sure to include these outstanding team members: Sherri Crandall, Sommer Crayton, Laura Crosby, Doug Drake, J.L. Martin, Dale Skram, and Karla Marie Williams. We are blessed beyond words. Thank you Jesus for these faith-filled and talented team members!

Many thanks to our publisher: Bold Vision Books. Karen, George, and Ginny working with you has been a pleasure! Thanks for sharing our excitement and our message!

Big appreciation to our editors, Deb Strubel and Katie McDivitt.

Last but never least, we are grateful for the love and support from our families. Our combined kids: Eric, Courtney, Jake, Kendra, Ryan, and Samantha. And our guys: Scott and Tom.

To the One who makes all things possible, Jesus Christ— the Author and Perfecter of Big Love.

With faith, hope, and love,
Lori & Becky

INTRODUCTION

LOVE IS HEART WORK

When I was a child, I talked like a child, I thought like a
child, I reasoned like a child.
When I became a man, I put childish ways behind me.

1 Corinthians 13:11

MATTERS OF THE HEART

"How many of you are amazed by the love you feel for your child?" I (Lori) asked the group of parents before me. All the hands in the room went up—including my own. "How many of you are shocked to discover you have a temper?" Laughter erupted and most of the hands went up again. I raised my hand again, too.

Becky and I know the heights and depths of emotion a parent experiences. We are moms, too.

One mom with a four-year-old daughter confessed, "I hate being a mom, and I don't like my kid!" She was frustrated and venting out. The bottom line was she was struggling with being a parent.

I (Lori) couldn't blame her. Her child was strong-willed plus highly creative. A tough kid to raise, no doubt. The little sugar-and-spice girl wasn't *so* nice. This child was ruling the roost. My heart ached for this mama. But I knew hope was within reach. Here she was, sitting in my parenting class, honestly expressing her feelings and ready and willing to learn. I'll be honest, there have been plenty of times I've been ready to turn in my mom badge, and I'm supposed to know what I'm doing. I recall my own mother saying she was going to change her name so we would stop calling out, "Mother!"

There are many child behaviors that are difficult for parents to address. Lots of those challenging issues are contained within the contents of this book. Becky and I will help you learn how to effectively and lovingly apply God's Word to everyday life with young kids. This book will show you how to do the following:

- ♥ Apply the four godly parenting styles for success
- ♥ Increase your child's self-worth by demonstrating patience
- ♥ Act in kindness to build family unity
- ♥ Foster sibling relationships rather than sibling rivalry
- ♥ Respond wisely when your child lies or steals
- ♥ Put respect back into the family
- ♥ Understand what drives your child's behavior
- ♥ Control your anger and effectively deal with conflict in the family
- ♥ Walk alongside your children when they are suffering
- ♥ Give your child strategies to deal with temptation
- ♥ Be your child's advocate in the school setting
- ♥ Support your gifted or special needs child
- ♥ Establish limits on media and technology
- ♥ Build a relationship with your children that will last a lifetime

We are confident as you read this book you will be a more successful mom or dad. Most importantly by loving *big*, 1 Corinthians 13 *big*, you will develop the kind of loving relationships with your children that will last a lifetime. (Note: For reasons of simplicity, we have chosen the masculine pronoun to represent any child throughout this book. We use the feminine pronoun only when the topic is mainly geared toward the female or the anecdote involves a female.)

Remember the first time you held your baby, making certain your precious bundle was swaddled just so, holding his head at the perfect angle? When did we stop feeling, "It's wonderful to be a parent!" and start saying to our spouse, "He's *your* son!"? When did we trade in our kid gloves for boxing gloves?

Becky and I think it *just* may have happened around the toddler time. Of course, if you had a colicky baby, you may have come to this point a little sooner. Toddlers move fast and have big opinions. It's like they consist of only wheels plus a mouth! (*Hmm.* Reminds me of the teen years.) Don't you hate that?

Once the child is more autonomous, moving and speaking on his own, life gets a little topsy-turvy. The undeniable fact Becky and I want to communicate is that parenting is hard work. Although lots of times parenting is the best job *ever*, other times the reality isn't what we dreamed it would be. One mom told me if she and her husband ever got a divorce, he would get the kids. She laughed as she said that, but we get the point.

There are times being a mom or dad isn't very much fun. Did the saying "the buck stops here" ever come to mind? Who gets to change that messy, leaking diaper? Who is going to get up with the sick child for the fifth time during the night? Who gets to clean that crusty little nose? Answer: Mom or Dad.

Most parents really love their children, love being a parent (on most days), and are doing their best. (Okay, I want to keep my mom badge.) Unfortunately, Becky and I have seen a trend where both moms and dads are unsure of their parenting abilities. That uncertainty, when coupled with a huge desire to parent perfectly, can lead to feelings of guilt and anxiety.

Newsflash: You will mess up. We all do. So get over the idea of perfectly raising a perfect kid. We are in good company, however. Think of Mary and Joseph. Even though they were parents of the perfect Son, they were imperfect parents. Can you believe they actually lost twelve-year-old Jesus and didn't even notice he was missing for a whole day? *Oops!* If there is anyone you'd want to keep track of, I'm thinking God's Son is the one. (Check it out the story in Luke 2:41–52.)

Messing up and not being perfect is okay. Having kids who do things the wrong way is to be expected. What is perfect is how our heavenly Father has put our families together. After all, He is in the family business!

So if you share the frustration of the mom at the beginning of this chapter, that's all right. In this book, we will help you work through some tough everyday stuff. Becky and I have done some things right and some things wrong. True confession: I've done lots wrong. So you may as well benefit from those mistakes. She and I share a common focus, a common faith, and a common desire to honor our Lord in the way we raise our kids. She's a mom with two sons, and I have three girls and a boy. We don't do things exactly the same, but we believe in the same principles. We want to encourage you and provide ideas and strategies that you can tailor to your own family.

Each family is unique, full of individual faults and idiosyncrasies. What is John Ortberg's saying? Something like, "Everyone is normal until you get to know them." All families have a little weirdness and dysfunction in them. Because of this, *The 1 Corinthians 13 Parent* series doesn't have a one-size-fits-all approach to family life. We are confident as you read this book and God's Word and apply the concepts presented according to your family's unique make-up, your parenting will be transformed.

By defining love, looking at our families of origin, and examining our favored parenting styles, we'll be receptive and ready to apply Paul's description of love in 1 Corinthians 13 in our families. If we love as the Lord loves, then love will never fail.

Love Is

- ♥ Love is patient, love is kind—a decision.

- ♥ It does not envy, it does not boast, it is not proud—an attitude.

- ♥ It is not rude, it is not self-seeking—outward focus.

- ♥ It is not easily angered, it keeps no record of wrongs—self-control.

- ♥ Love does not delight in evil but rejoices with the truth—a heavenly perspective.

♥ It always protects, always trusts—an action.

♥ It always hopes, always perseveres—a commitment.

♥ Love never fails—ultimate strength.

Love changes families. When you understand God's love, it will change you and how you relate to your kids. Then it will change how your kids relate to you and to each other.

Two years have passed since the mom at the beginning of this chapter shared her feelings. I'm elated to say she has learned effective strategies to raise her high-spirited youngster. Things aren't perfect, but they have improved greatly. *Woo-hoo!* She is keeping her mom badge. Her relationship with her daughter is strong. As the mom, she is back in charge, and her daughter has responded by being more cooperative. Fun has reentered the family.

No Strings

True love is unconditional. If we choose to love only when a child behaves or performs to our specifications, then we will be let down, and our child will believe love is something that is earned. Unconditional love is love without exceptions. No strings attached. No exclusions.

We concede it's difficult to love during a toddler's tantrum or a young child's persistent demands. Becky and I get that! Our kids have had tantrums and stubborn streaks, too.

Kids can drive you crazy. Like the mom mentioned earlier, as parents we can get so angry we may even feel as if we don't like the child. (By the way, that is normal.) That's why Jesus pointed out, "If you love those who love you, what credit is that to you? Even sinners love those who love them" (Luke 6:32). God loves us at our worst, and that's when we need His love the most. That's our model. Unconditional love provides stability for the child and is like God's love for His children. It helps to keep in mind that our children do not talk, think, or reason like adults. Okay, so we love them *even* when they act like kids!

GLANCING BACK

Before we talk in-depth about parenting, we want to reflect on our childhoods. Becky and I start many of our parenting classes with a quick family of origin assessment. We do this because it gives parents the opportunity to identify favorable and unfavorable family patterns. Sinful patterns are passed along from one generation to the next unless the chain is broken. Your family history has an impact on your present family.

The following assessment has ten questions. It asks where we have been and helps show what old tapes may be playing in our heads when we parent. Becky always encourages the participants in her classes to start the assessment with a quiet time of prayer, asking God to open their eyes, hearts, and minds. This is the best way to begin. Then, as you read, reflect on your family of origin and its relationships, faith, values, discipline methods, communication patterns, generational sins, and division of labor. We all bring these experiences into our parenting in the form of unspoken expectations. Warning: Ponder these questions with caution. This exercise isn't meant to be a blame game but a tool for recognizing the good and tossing the bad.

1 CORINTHIANS 13 PARENT:
RAISING LITTLE KIDS WITH BIG LOVE
FAMILY OF ORIGIN ASSESSMENT

1. Growing up, how were mistakes handled in your family (frustration, blame, patience, etc.)?

2. How was faith taught and lived in your family of origin?

3. Who made the major decisions in your home?

4. How would you describe the type of discipline your father used (train, punish, ignore, etc.)?

5. How would you describe your mother's approach to discipline?

6. How would you characterize your relationships with your siblings?

7. How was conflict dealt with in your family?

8. How were emotions expressed (freely, with restraint, repressed, etc.)?

9. What positive things would you like to pass along to your children from your upbringing?

10. What negative patterns from your upbringing would you like to change or avoid?

Expectations drive how we want our kids to act and who we think they should become. Expectations are good when it comes to desiring good behavior, but we need to tread carefully when it comes to personal choices like interests or hobbies. We also can have the false expectation that our children will love us back the same way we love them. *I went through fifteen hours of labor for you. You better love me,* we think. Or we think, *I hung in there and waited for you for two years before the adoption came through, so I desire some respect.* Remember that woes don't equal the love owed.

Here's something I think is really odd. In doing a biblical study on parental love, I have never found a verse that said children should love their parents. That doesn't seem right, does it? (If you find such a verse, please let me know.) The Bible does say kids should respect and honor their parents. But there is no mention of children being commanded to love Mom and Dad other than the general command to "love God and love others."

We, as moms and dads, have the expectation that because we love our children so much and have sacrificed greatly for them, they will do as they are told. Seems like a good trade-off. (Hmm. Maybe that's why Jesus said in John 14:23, "Anyone who loves me will obey my teaching.") What a surprise we get when our children acquire language and find power in the word "no". Uncooperative kids are difficult to live with.

Lack of cooperation in children and different family values between spouses are areas for potential conflict. Becky had such a couple in one of her classes. The dad told the participants how he and his wife struggled with discipline issues. Apparently, the wife was raised in a family where the girls were expected to be quiet and obedient while the boys were allowed to be rambunctious and bend the rules. (Truthfully, gals, wouldn't you have hated that?) The dad's childhood experience was a direct contrast. Growing up in his family, rules were rules for both the boys and the girls. Each parent naturally, and unconsciously, was drawn to the method used in their family of origin. This had conflict written all over it.

Because of the class and subsequent conversations, the couple became aware of their differing parenting expectations. They were able to come up with a mode of discipline that better fit their nuclear family. They began to work as a team as they raised their children. I'm sure their daughters appreciated that.

As we look back at our past, we want to remember we're not fault-finding. Most parents have the best intentions when raising their children. Even your own parents did. Our individual histories and expectations give us important insights into our present condition, as long as we take time to examine them.

Ebb and Flow

As our kids move from toddlers to preschoolers to elementary students, we adjust our expectations and parenting approaches accordingly. At least we ought to. It's tough to shift parenting styles when we are comfortable with one way. Know your child's abilities, and then parent to his age, stage, and personality.

As our children age, it is helpful to identify the approach we typically use and explore how to weave other techniques into the parenting mix. There are positives and negatives to each approach. Becky and I like to divide approaches to parenting into six categories: Controller, Chum, Coach, Consultant, Clueless, and Checked-Out. Typically, parents of younger kids will fall into the Controller or Chum categories. These two styles are both highly involved. The Controller is parent-centered while the Chum is child-centered. As the child ages and gains experience, integrating the training elements of the Coach into the Controller or Chum is a positive technique. It's unlikely the Consultant approach will be useful with children ages two to nine.

Watch for drawbacks when you overuse of any one technique. The biggest pitfall of the Chum category is having a whiny, demanding child who will then turn disrespectful with age. Not good! The negative effect reaped from using only a Controller style is that your parent-child relationship is behavior- and performance-based, making love and affection conditional. At first this seems good, at least on the surface, because the children are doing what they are told. Things externally look fine, while internally a fire is raging. As a parent with the default style of Controller, I (Lori) need to be aware of my parenting tendency. I like to blame my controlling tendencies on being a former teacher.

The upside to the Chum approach is that the child feels loved and shares enjoyable times with that parent. If your family goes to the pool, then being the Chum is appropriate until a safety concern arises. Then the Controller is needed. The positive aspect of the Controller is the child feels secure and safe. Both approaches in the right balance at the right time meet the child's basic needs of belonging and security. The Chum douses the emotional fire, and the Controller squelches the disrespect.

GOOD COMBO

In combining the Controller and Chum styles, there will be rules with relationship and then respect will reign in the family. After both love and limits are established, it is easier to transition into the Coach and

Consultant modes of parenting when kids get older. Parenting takes on different faces for different stages. Once we hold that baby in our arms, we're committed for the long haul. Our children need both love and limits.

Look at the following chart. Read over the characteristics of each of the various parenting styles. Each type described is exaggerated as a caution not to overuse any one technique. Examine the descriptions and determine which one is your default style, the style that tends to dominate your parenting.

1 CORINTHIANS 13 PARENT: RAISING LITTLE KIDS WITH BIG LOVE PARENTING STYLES CHART

RELATIONSHIP-BASED CHILD-FOCUSED

THE CHUM
"I WANT TO BE MY CHILD'S BEST FRIEND."

VALUES:	child's happiness, friendship with parent
PARENT BEHAVIOR:	high degree of warmth, acceptance, responsive, undemanding, indulgent, indecisive, weak, power relinquished, rescues, unable to say no, whines, begs, pleads, highly involved, makes excuses for child
FEAR:	conflict, doesn't want child to get upset
DISCIPLINE STRATEGY:	permissive
NEGATIVE RESULT:	child is dependent, disrespectful, whiny, manipulative, demanding, insecure, resentful
POSITIVE RESULT:	child feels loved, knows he belongs

The Consultant
"I'm here to advise."

Values:	child's decision-making skills, maturity, independence
Parent Behavior:	actively observes, listens, evaluates, imparts wisdom when asked, may ask permission to give advice
Fear:	wonders if child is ready for this. Asks self, "Have I said too little or too much?"
Discipline Strategy:	allows natural consequences to be the teacher, asks questions
Negative Result:	child may flounder and make lots of mistakes
Positive Result:	child is independent, responsible, confident, knows parent is there for support

The Clueless
"I blindly trust my child."

Values:	child's independence and maturity
Parent Behavior:	overwhelmed or stressed, weak, warm, relies on belief child is always good, unable to keep promises, uninformed, relies heavily on others to help raise child, undemanding, appears laid back, confused, blames others for child's behavior, feels helpless
Fear:	"I won't know what to do, or I'll be more overwhelmed if I engage."
Discipline Strategy:	threatens but ultimately does nothing, avoids discipline
Negative Result:	child is rebellious, angry, prone to aggressive behavior, disrespectful, seeks structure, doesn't feel capable
Positive Result:	child may become a risk-taker and is resourceful.

| RULES-BASED |
| PARENT-FOCUSED |

THE CONTROLLER
"I'M IN CHARGE."

VALUES:	order and good behavior
PARENT BEHAVIOR:	forceful, decisive, highly organized, controlling, demanding, overbearing, micro-manager, authoritarian, highly involved, points, preaches, threatens, instills guilt, takes over
FEAR:	loss of control, lack of respect
DISCIPLINE STRATEGY:	punishment
NEGATIVE RESULT:	child is dependent, resistant, rebellious, withdrawn, blames others, lies, sneaky
POSITIVE RESULT:	child feels safe and secure

THE COACH
"I'm here to guide and lead."

VALUES:	family unity, rules, interdependence, cooperation, commitment, connection
PARENT BEHAVIOR:	encourages and supports child in struggles, provides solutions, sets limits, authoritative, responsive, demanding, actively involved, able to make the tough call
FEAR:	loss of family unity
DISCIPLINE STRATEGY:	prevention, training, retraining, redirecting
NEGATIVE RESULT:	child may lose some autonomy and individuality due to the family focus
POSITIVE RESULT:	child feels capable, lovable, secure, accountable, responsive, respectful, cooperative

THE CHECKED OUT
"I'm busy."

VALUES:	own personal time and schedule
PARENT BEHAVIOR:	busy, workaholic, distracted, may try to buy love with material items, unattached or disconnected, strong-willed parent, cold, uninvolved, unavailable, self-absorbed
FEAR:	child will be dependent
DISCIPLINE STRATEGY:	none unless a big problem, then jumps to extreme punishment
NEGATIVE RESULT:	child is withdrawn, seeks attention from other adults, may try to prove worth through achievement, defeatist attitude, doesn't feel loved
POSITIVE RESULT:	child is self-reliant and resourceful

Note that the four styles—Chum, Controller, Coach, and Consultant—have more positive results for the child than the two—Clueless and Checked Out. Parents typically use a combination of styles but tend toward one particular category most often. The overuse of any style or misuse of a style in a particular situation produces the negative results.

The last two mentioned in each category, Clueless and Checked Out, are largely to be avoided, so we will not focus on those methods. Within the chapters that follow, we will offer positive and negative examples of the four desirable styles. These scenarios will give life to the descriptions listed in the chart. If you had trouble identifying yourself in the chart, then you may have an easier time after you've read all the scenarios.

The Mix

The combination of our childhood experiences in our families of origin and our personal default parenting style factors into the way we raise our children. Being aware of patterns and subtle influences is the first step to parenting well.

Each section within the book focuses on one of the fifteen virtues of love as presented in 1 Corinthians 13. By implementing each quality of love, parenting approaches will be more effective, good character in kids will develop, and God will be honored in the process.

Take what you have learned from your past, accentuate the positives, and alter the negatives. Love God and love your family members without condition and without exception. This is the love that Paul describes in 1 Corinthians 13. In his letter to the people in Corinth, Paul laid out "the most excellent way" (1 Corinthians 12:31b). Love is a choice.

Prayer

Holy God,
Thank You that You are my perfect parent. Thank You for the blessing of my earthly parents. Help me to pass along generational traits that are honoring to You, and free me

from those that are sinful. I ask that You will be Lord of my life and my home. Please be my ever-present guide and counselor as I raise the children with whom You have blessed me. Please forgive me when I fall short. Give me the eyes to see and the humility to correct poor parenting habits. Thank You for being my Abba, daddy, and my friend.

In the precious name of Jesus,

Amen

AND YET I WILL SHOW YOU THE MOST EXCELLENT WAY.

1 Corinthians12:31b

SECTION ONE

LOVE IS A DECISION

Chapter 1

Choose Patience

Love is patient

1 Corinthians 13:4a

Predictably Unpredictable

We are excited to share something with you. There are fifteen attributes of love in 1 Corinthians 13. The list begins with patience. "So what?" you say. This is a *huge* revelation. Patience is listed first because it is the most important one. The other fourteen hinge on the virtue of patience.

That's kind of a good news–bad news piece of information. Pre-parent, I (Lori) considered myself to be a patient person. Kids, my own kids, have been the true test of that. And I've failed the patience test on many occasions. Here's my theory: Patience is much more difficult when we are passionate about the people involved and are highly invested in the outcome. That typifies parenting. No wonder most parents pray for patience.

I used to pray for patience, too. But what I really wanted was for things to go smoothly. It's easy to be patient when things run like clockwork. It is much more difficult when we feel annoyed, embarrassed, inconvenienced, or challenged. "Help the weak, be patient with everyone" (1 Thessalonians 5:14c). Patience is the virtue needed when things don't go as planned.

Life with kids is unpredictable. Here are a few scenarios that have played out in my home.

A child fully dressed and equipped for the school day has the urge to use the bathroom just as it's time to catch the bus. Missing the bus is the result. Mother Nature won't be hurried.

Another child leaves ABC (*already been chewed*) gum in a pocket, which goes undetected as it enters the wash and results in a dryer webbed with the sticky substance. (I'm going to take a wild guess and say Becky has never had the pleasure of picking gum out of the dryer. I'm thinking she's a pocket checker.)

A child spikes a fever on Christmas Eve. Holiday plans are canceled.

Some problems can be prevented, like the gummy dryer. Others, not. No matter. Patience is the virtue of love called for in unexpected or annoying circumstances.

In Scripture, patience is often paired with the words *endurance* and *wisdom*. Steadfastly and thoughtfully responding to challenging circumstances characterizes a patient person. No matter your personality, family history, or current circumstances, you can increase your patience and develop the trait in kids. Patience is a matter of the will, a choice.

With less irritation comes less impatience. When kids cooperate, adult frustration is reduced. So, we are going to change the things we can change. We'll implement some positive prevention strategies by effectively communicating with our children so they are more agreeable. We will examine typical parent-child power struggles over eating, toileting, and sleeping. Demonstrating patience while training children in a new task and waiting before speaking are ways to build confidence in kids. Let's parent deliberately to increase patience in ourselves and our kids.

> **PATIENCE IS A MATTER OF THE WILL, A CHOICE.**

In 'n' Out

"Why is it so hard to get out the door?"

"I get so frustrated when it's time to leave and my child throws a fit."

"Getting my child into his car seat is an aerobic exercise."

These are typical frustrations shared by parents of young kids. Transitions are hard for kids, hard on parents.

Look at the Two Different Styles

"Alex, it's time to go. We're leaving," one mom declares while turning off Alex's favorite TV program.

"Alex, we need to leave in five minutes. Get ready to shut your show off in five minutes," says a different mom.

The first scenario is the negative version of the parent as Controller. The approach is abrupt and lacks sensitivity. In the second example, the parent is still in charge, but the words are issued in kindness and some control is released to the child. Of course, in using the second approach the parent must mean what he is saying. When five minutes is up, it is time to go. We all appreciate a bit of a warning before changing gears. This often prevents the transition tantrum.

One mom expressed frustration over trying to get her six-year-old son to clean up his Legos before leaving the house. "Our rule is to clean up the toys before we leave the house," she said. "Joey practically goes into convulsions each time he has to put his Legos away. This *really* tries my patience!"

We discussed allowing her son to have a spot where he could keep his unfinished projects. Then he would know he could return to his work later. Joey's mom hadn't realized how important it was for him to complete what he started. He was creating, not playing. Once she implemented this change, leaving home was no longer a problem.

When impatience and frustration stir in parent or child, it's time to develop a plan.

Deal with It

Parenting a child who needs to touch everything in sight can drive a parent crazy. Kids with a tactile learning style must touch, smell, or taste new objects. The absence of a hands-on experience increases the child's irritability. This type of kid needs to behave like this to successfully process new information. I (Lori) have a tactile child. Her goal isn't to get under my skin. She wants to learn, and she knows how she learns best.

I recall moving some new furniture into my daughter's room when she was three years old. She had to touch *everything*. I felt exasperated, "Why do you keep touching everything?"

"I have to touch it," she said. "Then I feel comfortable."

Her statement captures a tactile kid's need to physically handle new things in order to fully understand them.

Shopping with a tactile little one is an exercise in patience. Here's an approach I found helpful; I hope it can help you, too. "I know you need to touch the buttons," I'd say, for example. "You can touch them *after* we finish our errands. Until then, keep your hands in your pockets." Of course, I did need to be respectful and make certain the button pushing later would not be a problem for the establishment.

In providing some perimeters for touching, many things are accomplished. The child and parent will both feel less frustrated. The child's need for physical experience and the parent's need for speed will both be met. I promise this phase will not last forever. Soon the ability to generalize experiences will start and the need to touch everything will become less frequent. Who knows? You may have a little engineer on your hands!

Certain types of clothing or material can present another frustration for tactile kids or highly sensitive children and their parents.

40

One mom shared how her nine-year-old daughter would go into all sorts of contortions while putting on a pair of jeans. "She scratches her bottom, puts her arms into her pant legs, and stretches the fabric away from her body. Then she goes into a full body squirm."

Apparently, the little girl preferred sweatpants to jeans, but her mom favored jeans. The mother wondered if her child was attempting to manipulate her by behaving this way. That is unlikely. There are two more plausible explanations. The child could be prepubescent and a little thicker around the middle so the elastic waistband of the sweatpants is more comfortable, or this little gal is highly sensitive to textures.

This is one of those times that I say, "This doesn't have to be a problem. Jeans or sweats? Both are casual clothes. Allow the sweats. If jeans versus sweats is a power struggle, then take away the power by not making a big deal over the article of clothing. If she's developing, she probably feels too confined in the jeans. If it's a sensitivity issue, then you'll want to accommodate the sweatpants request."

Kids who are highly sensitive to sounds, smells, and textures need special consideration. Give your child a coping tool. If smells bothers him, then have him plug his nose or move away from the odor. If loud noises are problematic, then teach him to cover his ears or allow him to wear earphones and listen to music. If textures are irritating, then cut off clothing tags, check for protruding seams, and avoid buying clothes that will make him itchy and uncomfortable. Do your best to work with the idiosyncrasies of your youngster. Over time, your child will develop other coping mechanisms to get through the day.

> **KIDS WITH A TACTILE LEARNING STYLE MUST TOUCH, SMELL, OR TASTE NEW OBJECTS.**

FOOD FIGHT

Kids have preferences in the way they take in information and in the type of food they ingest. "No, Mommy!" they may say. "No icky brown stuff." When my (Becky) son was little, he was opposed to icky brown stuff (chocolate)! Hard to believe, I know. Some kids decide they won't eat anything green. Others determine they will only eat a few certain foods, cooked a particular way.

Here's a secret. Kids have total control over three things: falling asleep, using the toilet, and swallowing food. And they know it. Armed with this information, the parent has a choice: Enter into a power struggle in which losing is certain, or decide to control what can be controlled.

If the issue is food, think of the things that you can influence: food purchased, food cooked, food offered. A new food may need to be offered up to fifteen times before some children will even try it. Don't push food. Demonstrate good eating habits and show enjoyment of all items without placing a higher value on one food over another. Avoid saying, "If you eat your broccoli, then you can have dessert." The subtle message is, "Put up with the nasty broccoli so you can reach the desired goal of dessert." Just keep putting the broccoli on the table. Some foods are an acquired taste.

One mom was exhausted from making a variety of entrées for her fussy eater. This poor woman had put herself in the position of being a short-order cook with her darling youngster as the demanding customer. This mama needed to take back the reins.

Limited options for breakfast, lunch, and snack time are okay. For instance, picking a cereal or choosing a fruit. For the evening meal, get in the practice of one dinner for one family, made by one cook.

I (Becky) recommended the breakfast-is-next tactic to the frazzled mom. If a child doesn't like a certain food, then he can choose to skip it by saying, "No, thank you." If the child completely rejects the meal, then state, "After dinner comes breakfast. Breakfast is next." Then stick to the policy, and don't give in and allow a snack or meal substitute.

If your children are not thriving, have a growth concern or a health issue, then you won't want to take this approach. Usually finicky eaters don't eat a good dinner because they know they can finagle something later. Some kids are not hungry because they snack all day.

Becky and I get many questions regarding a healthy diet. We remind parents that pediatricians assure us most kids actually get what they need. Many kids eat only one good meal a day. If you're concerned, then check with the doctor and give a children's vitamin each day.

Having a meal at someone else's home can be stressful. A technique to use to avoid the embarrassing declaration, "I don't like that!" would be to instruct your kids, prior to the visit, to put a little of everything on their plates. Food not touching other foods, of course! Then eat only what is appealing.

Once the child realizes he can't control your mood with his food choices, the battle dissipates. Food issues tend to be more about power than preference. Don't let mealtime become a struggle.

> ## ONCE THE CHILD REALIZES HE CAN'T CONTROL YOUR MOOD WITH HIS FOOD CHOICES, THE BATTLE DISSIPATES.

BEDTIME BOOMERANG

Bedtime is a relief after a long day—for the parents. You put the kids to bed, plop down on the couch, and exhale. Your muscles begin to relax. Then your little guy sheepishly peeks around the corner. Good thing for him, he is so cute in his jammies. You take a big breath and feel your muscles tighten. It's going to be a long night.

What is the best response? Haul that little rascal back to his room; strictly businesslike. Establish a nighttime routine: bathe, brush teeth, read a story, say prayers, give a kiss, sip water, and turn off the light. Consistently stick to the plan. When the nighttime ritual is done, don't revisit any of the routine. Have a pre-sleep list so your child can check off the things completed. When the child has trouble falling asleep, difficulty adjusting to a big bed, or has a fear of separation, he seeks out his mom and dad. Usually, he isn't a welcome sight.

Some kids need extra time to settle down. Having a bedtime basket of books or non-choke-able toys and a special nighttime buddy, like a *very sleepy* stuffed animal, can help keep your young child in bed. If the post-bedtime appearance becomes a pattern, try this: Pick a night when you feel up to dealing with the issue. Do the bedtime routine. As you leave the bedroom, say, "Stay in bed. I'll be back to check on you in five minutes." If the bedtime boomerang is due to separation issues or fear, knowing you'll return will help. Look in on him when five minutes is up. Continue to do this throughout the evening, increasing the time between visits. Each time, look in the room and state, "I will be back soon." The next night, make your first check-in time longer than the previous night. This process takes a while but is usually successful.

Other parents let their child cry it out. One mom who used this strategy said they had two agonizing nights of sobbing, but now they are over the hump. She was satisfied with the results of the tough approach. Pick the strategy that fits your family.

There are a few practices we have observed that we want to address. We are not in the camp of having no bedtime, lying with the child till he falls asleep, or having a family bed. (That being said, some families don't see these strategies as problematic.) Having a specific bedtime, learning how to settle oneself, and private mom and dad space are all important, in our opinion. We can almost see the dads nodding in agreement to the last thought. If your little one makes an occasional nighttime visit, keep a sleeping bag or pallet under your bed. He can pull out his gear and fall asleep on the floor next to your bed. Keeping your child in bed can be a process.

POTTY TALK

Becky and I have wondered if there is some toilet training conspiracy. Why doesn't someone let parents know potty training can be a *thing*? Some kids get it right away; for others it drags on *forever*. In my family, we had both extremes. We had every type of potty chair imaginable: a portable mini-toilet, one that attaches to the existing commode complete with little steps, another that could be placed on the seat at a moment's notice. Good equipment is helpful, but it is up to the child to use it.

Think of all the things that affect training: emotions, language development, social awareness, and physical control. The parents' attitude plays a big role also. Lots of experts say parents must be consistent. Here's where you can breathe a sigh of relief. No, you don't have to be. Consistency in potty training may be impossible.

A dry diaper following a nap is the best indicator your child is physically capable. If he expresses an interest in using the toilet, then that is a good sign he's ready. Take your child on a special mission to pick out big kid underwear. Becky's boys chose character undies. They never wanted to poop on Spidey!

Choose a time of day you tend to be at home. For us it was the afternoon. Be patient. Be positive. Don't punish. Try not to feel pressure from other parents experiencing success. It's not a competition. On days you feel especially tired, skip the training and put a diaper on the child. Better to have a good attitude and lots of patience than to be consistent and cranky. Rest assured, your child will get it.

LUMPY BEDS

Our fast-paced way of life impacts our ability to properly train our kids. We generally want things done fast and finished in a specific way. When we're not satisfied with the process or outcome, impatience may result. In our rush to have a task completed, we may take over our children's jobs. In order for our children to learn, they must do some tasks without our intervention.

Take the supposedly simple job of making a bed. I (Becky) thought this would be an easy task to teach my five-year-old son.

"Okay, Buddy, here is how you do it." I began in Controller form, showing him how to stretch the fitted sheet, pull up the flat sheet, tuck in the quilt, and straighten the pillows.

"Now it's your turn to try" (Coach).

He mimicked my actions. The result was *okay*.

The next day, I poked my head in his room to check on the bed-making. The flat sheet was the lump at the foot of the bed, the quilt was haphazardly pulled across, and the pillows were thrown on in disarray.

"Well, I'll quickly fix this." The Controller had returned in extreme form.

The third day of the week, I reminded my son to make his bed.

"Mom, will you do it for me?"

"Why?" I asked.

"If I do it wrong, you'll redo it."

Touché! I never should have redone his work. My son felt inadequate.

Together, we gave it another shot. I put the Controller to bed and exercised a combo of the Coach and Chum techniques. The next morning, I found his bed neater but still a little lumpy. This time I resisted the urge to fix it.

There is a tremendous sense of satisfaction in starting and finishing a job. When training children to do work around the house, model perseverance and self-control. Impatience is shown not only through anger and frustration but also in taking over, redoing, and fixing. Parental restraint coupled with the child's determination to do the job well will build the child's patience and confidence. Colossians 3:12b encourages us clothe ourselves with patience.

> ### ALLOW YOUR CHILDREN THE SATISFACTION OF STARTING AND COMPLETING A JOB.

SPEAK UP

As parents we may move to action or words more quickly than we ought. As Solomon said, "[There is] a time to be silent and a time to speak" (Ecclesiastes 3:7b). Waiting through the awkward silence as our kids formulate an answer to a question an adult asks takes a lot of self-control. We're given many opportunities to encourage our children's confidence and maturity by remaining quiet. As a disclaimer, there are some children who are comfortable speaking up and will monopolize conversations. If your young one takes over, then train him in conversational give-and-take. If his tendency is to hold back, then allow times for him to speak.

One parent shared a great technique she used with her child. She would pass a wooden spoon to her child when it was his turn to speak. When he was done talking, he'd pass the spoon back. Becky also recommends a little jumpstart for the quieter ones. "Johnny," she says, "tell about the time you went fishing."

There are risks that come when a parent is being quiet and allowing the child to speak. Inaccuracy and embarrassment are two downsides that come to mind.

"When do you bathe?" the pediatrician asked my (Lori) nine-year-old daughter.

"On Thursdays."

The pediatrician made a notation on the chart.

I smiled to myself. My daughter bathed more often than once a week, but she was thinking about a specific day due to the way she interpreted the question. Following her Thursday horseback-riding lessons, she had to shower. Her response was accurate, just not complete.

The doctor never asked me for clarification, and I didn't give any. She directed the question to my child, and the question had been answered. If this had been an important health issue, then I would have clarified. But it wasn't. Also, if I didn't have a personal relationship with the doctor, I would have spoken up. I trusted this doctor. This was a safe opportunity for my young child to speak for herself. I *have* wondered what was recorded in her file.

It's hard for me to hold back. My responses are more accurate, clear, and concise. But that's not the point. Children need to speak for themselves. Let's encourage each other to be slow to speak so our kids can develop their own voice.

> **WE'RE GIVEN MANY OPPORTUNITIES TO ENCOURAGE OUR CHILDREN'S CONFIDENCE AND MATURITY BY REMAINING QUIET.**

EENIE MEENIE

Children have many opportunities for making decisions, from a preschooler choosing what clothes to wear to a school-aged child deciding in which extra-curricular activity to be involved.

Allow for some decision making when your children are young. Toddlers are able to make decisions. They have big opinions! By giving a choice of two things, with either option being acceptable to the parent, little ones have an opportunity to have limited control over a situation. This is a great strategy if your child is in the doing-by-self phase. For example, in the winter, a parent may say, "You can choose your red or blue mittens." Either choice is okay with the parent. Usually, the child will pick red or blue.

There are the little rascals that will say, "Green."

The next appropriate parental response is to reiterate the choice: "Red, blue, or I'll pick." The child, not wanting to relinquish power, should go back to the original choice of two. If this doesn't occur, then choose for the child.

There's a caution with the choice approach. Don't overuse it. If this strategy is used many times throughout the day, your child will lose confidence in your ability to make decisions. He'll also grow weary from having to make so many decisions. Use choices sparingly.

USE CHOICES SPARINGLY.

PATIENT PROCESS

"This is the year of patience," a mom and dad declared. While they were increasing their ability to respond with patient restraint, their two boys were also beginning to develop patience. The parents' patient approach made a positive impact on the children.

When the parents model patience, children begin to develop more patience. When parents are supportive and stop themselves from taking over in word and deed, they discover their children's self-worth increases. As self-worth increases, frustration decreases. The end results are confidence and contentment. The byproducts of patient parenting are not bad for parent or child.

Love Notes on Patience

Lori writes: I think most impatient actions are born out of frustration. I have a child with a learning disability. She would get so frustrated she *literally* tore her hair out. She had a bald spot the size of a quarter on the side of her head for about a year. So if you are like me and have a child with a disability, be aware that his basket is already full. Approach new learning in smaller chunks so more success and less frustration are experienced.

Becky writes: I'm most impatient when I'm tired. The same is true for my kids. Most kids and parents are short on sleep. It sounds so simple, but getting enough rest makes all the difference. Perspectives change. Irritability, frustration, and impatience decrease. Really, everything *is* better in the morning.

Questions

1. Describe a common parent-child power struggle. What can you control? How can you change the dynamics?

2. When have you been patient in the midst of a frustrating situation?

3. How do you handle times of transition in your home?

Parenting Tips

1. Avoid getting into a power struggle over toilet training, eating, and sleeping.

2. Resist the urge to redo a job you've given your child.

3. Use the choice approach sparingly.

Prayer

Father,

Please grant me wisdom so I may exercise patience as I raise the children You have given me. Give me discerning eyes so I can understand why my children behave the way they do. Help me to be sensitive to circumstances that trigger frustration. Give me the strength to lead in love, a love that begins with patience.

Amen

PATIENCE IS BETTER THAN PRIDE.

Ecclesiastes 7:8b

Chapter 2

Choose Kindness

Love is kind.

1 Corinthians 13:4b

Kindness Quest

We have observed a cultural inclination toward unkindness. Unkindness is commonplace among family members. Not just between siblings but between Mom and Dad and between parent and child. Phrases like "I'm not gonna lie" or "I'll be honest" precede a nasty comment. As if brutal honesty makes unkind words acceptable.

Quick clever quips have replaced sensitive sentiments. An attitude of fierce independence and a misunderstood approach to teaching responsibility is pushing kindness out of the home and out of our society.

We seem to be saying, "Handle it yourself. It's your problem." That seems pretty harsh to me (Lori). Shouldn't we be there for each other? Moms and dads, let's up our game in terms of caring for each other in the family. Kindness is the quality of love that brings unity, knitting us together. The lack of it will tear families apart.

I'll admit I have trouble doling out kindness. My tongue can be sharp. I know how to wield it. That's why I'm writing the main portion of this chapter. I'm hoping (so is my husband) I'll take the information to heart.

In looking at 1 Corinthians 13, I noticed a comma is the only thing that separates patience and kindness. To be kind, patience must come first. A patient person has the ability to persevere, and the kind person is able to act and speak with love.

With God's help, we can bring kindness back into our families. When we practice empathy and gentleness, kindness returns. Let's make kindness reappear in society one word, one act, one home at a time.

A Kind Environment

"Be kind and compassionate to one another" (Ephesians 4:32a). Kindness takes a little extra energy, thought, and a dose of self-control. Parents set the tone. If we want our children to be kind to each other, then we need to intentionally model and reinforce kind actions and words.

When someone spilled something at my home, I got in the habit of saying, "That's okay. Everybody spills. I'll help you clean it up." I repeated those three statements often throughout the day when my four kids were younger. (Like, *really* often!) Sometimes those words helped me get through the moment more than they helped the spiller. The message I conveyed to the kids was one of grace, empathy, humility, and helpfulness. The fruit of regularly using this technique is when we parents hear one sibling say to another, "That's okay. Everybody spills. I'll help you clean it up." Isn't that better than saying, "You are so careless; you spilled your milk. You need to clean it up!"?

Many proponents of natural consequences would disagree with this approach. They would recommend having the child clean up the spill alone in order to experience personal responsibility. But we can do better than that. Let's raise the bar from training our kids to be responsible to showing them how to extend love and grace while building relationships through kind acts. We demonstrate love when we help each other. Ultimately, don't we want our kids to be able to count on us and on one another after they have just metaphorically spilled?

Acts of Kindness

Kindness in deed looks like helpfulness. Kindness in words feels like empathy or encouragement. Kindness flows naturally from the highly relational Chum. If you tend toward the Controller style like I do, then be intentional about integrating kindness into your parenting. Maybe you can include doing a favor for your young one in your day. By combining the parental example of speaking and acting kindly with the expectation of kind interactions among family members, you will help foster unity.

Kind actions result in respect for the receiver and doer. "A kindhearted woman gains respect" (Proverbs 11:16a). Becky and I came up with a list of actions that aren't hard to implement:

♥ Open the door for someone.

♥ Give up your seat to an older person or a pregnant woman.

♥ Allow someone with a few items to go ahead of you in the grocery store checkout line.

When we model these simple acts of kindness, our children will follow suit.

Even more important than random acts of kindness to a stranger are deliberate acts of kindness to family members. Little kids *want* to help. Let them. When my (Becky) boys were little they wanted to be kitchen assistants. My little guys would carry in the groceries and help unload the bags. Yes, we had squished bread and broken eggs, but I thought it was more important to support their willingness to help than to prevent food damage.

When dinnertime rolled around, the two of them asked for a chore. It would have been easier for me to do everything myself, but it was great having them involved. Setting the table was a perfect job for them. They took their table job so seriously that I sometimes needed to suppress a giggle.

"Mommy, does the fork go on this side or that side of the plate?"

"Do I use the big forks or the little forks?"

"Whoops! I dropped one."

"That one goes in the sink, please," I'd call out.

By allowing my sons to participate in dinnertime preparation, they felt as if they were an integral part of the process. When I thanked them for their assistance, the ideas of helping each other and working together were reinforced. They felt needed and began linking service and kindness together.

Kids helping parents and parents helping kids is family life at its best. If a child calls from school in need of an important forgotten item, then parents have a choice. We can take the logical consequence route and say, "Oh, bummer, so sorry. What will you do?" Or we can demonstrate grace and lend a hand. I (Lori) would feel abandoned if I needed help but it was withheld so I could "learn a lesson." Unless the child habitually forgets a particular thing, help him out if you are able.

We want our kids to look to the family for support. We hope our homes will be places where the members feel valued and loved. When we show kindness, consideration, and thoughtfulness, then long-lasting, positive family relationships are the result.

Just Kiddin'

The words we use have the power to bless or wound. Sarcasm or condescension is unkind. I (Lori) overheard a mom say to her four-year-old son, "What part of no don't you understand?" Kids are literal in nature. I wondered if he understood the question. If he did, what was his reaction supposed to be? His mom had belittled him and gave him no idea how to proceed. (I had to hold myself back. I really wanted to step in and provide some unsolicited advice. *Ah*, with kindness, of course.)

Shame and confusion are the results of a sarcastic comment. Instead, let's say what we mean, being direct and specific rather than hurtful. Little ones want to please. No need to be mean. "Encourage one another and build each other up" (1 Thessalonians 5:11a).

> THE WORDS WE CHOOSE TO USE HAVE
> THE POWER TO BLESS OR WOUND.

STICKS AND STONES

Ridiculing and laughing at someone is cruel and disrespectful. Remember the chant, "Sticks and stones can break my bones but words will never hurt me"? That's a big fat lie. Name-calling is mean-spirited and meant to harm. Directly teach empathy by having your child imagine himself in another's shoes. Although empathy is best learned through personal experiences, parents can foster compassion through discussion, demonstration, or role-playing.

When hurtful words are spoken, even in jest, deal with the situation. When my (Lori) children were preschool through early elementary age, I required that the offender who made a mean-spirited comment immediately say three nice things about the person he had insulted. Then I had the offender ask for forgiveness and follow up with a gentle hug or touch. As my kids matured, I upped the ante. Once children can automatically rattle off encouraging yet not heartfelt words, the discipline technique needs to be adjusted. The next step Tom and I took was to have the offending child write a note to the offended child. This note included three things he appreciated about the other. Prior to the note being delivered, it needed to pass the Dad or Mom Screening Test. That left little room for the note to be turned into something ugly.

Between siblings, sometimes hurtful actions take place, rather than hurtful words being spoken. When things get physical—pushing, shoving, hair pulling, etcetera—use the same techniques with a little different twist. With a toddler, quickly have him give three gentle touches to the person he just hurt. Repeat, "We use gentle touch in our family." With a preschool- or school-aged child, have the bully do three acts of service for the bullied. The victim gets to choose what those acts are in order for him to have power over the problem. These acts need to be completed in a short amount of time.

> **DIRECTLY TEACH EMPATHY BY HAVING YOUR CHILD IMAGINE HE IS IN ANOTHER'S SHOES.**

They can be as simple as getting the child a glass of juice or as involved as doing his chores for him. The three acts of kindness should be preceded by asking forgiveness and followed with a hug. Deal with the issues at hand in a short period of time.

THE OL' ONE-TWO

Becky and I think it's a miracle that most parents don't receive a broken nose, black eye, or sustain other injuries when parenting little kids. How many times have you been accidently conked, tripped, or stepped on? Kids seem to whip their heads up at the least opportune times, bonking Mom or Dad in the nose or under the chin. Physical pain is a part of the parenting experience. When pain is the result of an impulse or accident, that is, your child didn't mean to hurt you, then overlook it. But when intentional pain is inflicted, that is a completely different situation that requires immediate attention.

I'll (Becky) never forget the time my son bit me. He was snuggled into the nape of my neck, a nice mommy-child moment.

Suddenly, for no apparent reason, he bit me.

"Ouch!" I yelped. "Why did you do that?" Reasons for the bite ran through my mind, and I considered that it might have been a love bite.

I plopped him down on the floor immediately.

He burst into tears. His wide eyes and gaping mouth confirmed the bite wasn't meant to harm. He was as shocked as I was.

Biting surprises parents. It seems so animalistic. Who knows what goes through the child's mind pre-bite. Maybe the child is frustrated or teething: "My teeth are really aching, maybe if I clamp down here…." Maybe it's a little experiment: "I wonder what will happen if…." Or maybe the child thinks, "I just love Mommy so much I could just eat her up."

No matter the reason, the response should be the same. Say or exclaim, "No!" Put the child down, and add, "Mouths are for kissing. Give Mommy three gentle touches."

Biting, hitting, pinching, or any other inappropriate physical behavior from a toddler or preschooler is not alarming. They are common developmental behaviors that need to be extinguished. A school-aged child that uses physical force or intimidation around siblings or peers, however, has deeper issues. Our homes should be safe places for everyone. If you notice one child bullying another, then do not ignore this behavior. Try the three acts of kindness. Follow through with any punishment you have meted out. The victim child needs to know that the parent controls the home and the bully does not. If you continue to see a pattern of abusive behavior, get professional help. Ignoring this behavior will only exacerbate the problem.

A child hitting a parent is never acceptable. He is attempting to physically control you. Picture your child age ten, fifteen, or eighteen. One day he will most likely be bigger and stronger than both Mom and Dad. While you are still physically larger and more powerful, this is best the time to alter his behavior. Say, "Stop!" Then say, "You're frustrated (or angry). Use your words instead of hitting. Go to your room (or wherever the thinking spot is in the home). Think about how you will handle your anger differently the next time."

When he is ready with an answer, he can come back into the family fold. Have him tell you his plan, make it right by delivering three gentle touches or three acts of services, say he's sorry for hitting you, and then ask for forgiveness. Follow up the training with a big hug and an "I love you."

If hitting a parent is not dealt with, then it has the potential to increase. Hair pulling, head butting, kicking, punching, choking, and worse can emerge. Do not tolerate any physical abuse.

BIGGEST FAN

Teaching and exhibiting empathy are ways to increase the kindness factor. Having empathy for a child when he struggles promotes understanding. A parent sharing a story of a personal struggle reassures the child that challenges are a part of life. Kids love these stories. When my kids were little and had an "accident," they loved hearing about the time I accidently wet my pants. (Oh! This calls for clarification. I should add *as a little kid.*)

Not everything our kids do is going to be great. While we want to build up our homes with encouragement, we don't want to give false praise. "A wise woman builds her house, but with her own hands the foolish one tears hers down" (Proverbs 14:1). Keep encouraging words honest, and be specific with praise. Admit some things are hard and take longer to learn. False praise prevents children from striving to do better and gives them a false notion of themselves as greater than they are.

Look at the contrast in the following interactions. Compare the Controller's threat to the Coach's guidance.

The Controller states, "You aren't working very hard at learning to read. If your reading doesn't improve, you can't _____."

Upon hearing this the child will emotionally shut down. He will not be motivated to do better. He'll feel defeated and misunderstood. His personality will dictate if he feels shame or anger.

The Coach says, "I'm noticing that reading is challenging for you. It was hard for me, too. It looks like you need some help. I know you can do this. You're a smart kid. I'll help you."

Same problem, different message and delivery. The Controller is making an accusation that may or may not be true. Following the accusatory statement he makes a threat. The Coach, on the other hand, is not accusing or assuming but addressing the issue with empathy and encouragement. By factoring kindness into the equation, the child feels supported and loved. When he feels cared for rather than scolded and threatened, he will be more open to accept help.

When noticing a problematic area, begin with a kind approach. Use punishment as the last resort. Training kids moves them forward toward resolution; punishment sits in the past. Everyone has God-given talents and abilities. We all have God-allowed struggles. Sharing both our successes and challenges with our kids builds bridges of understanding, compassion, and empathy. Be your child's biggest fan!

> **SHARING BOTH SUCCESSES AND CHALLENGES WITH OUR KIDS BUILDS BRIDGES OF UNDERSTANDING, COMPASSION, AND EMPATHY.**

WHISPER

Gentleness is often associated with kindness in Scripture. Gentleness is seen as a strong quality. Proverbs 25:15 says, "A gentle tongue can break a bone." Gentle words have strength. Most of us prefer a gentle touch to a firm tug. Paul even asks the church at Corinth, "What do you prefer? Shall I come to you with a whip, or in love and with a gentle spirit?" (1 Corinthians 4:21).

When giving your child an instruction or a correction, use a gentle and quiet delivery. Move close to increase the importance and value of the message. The farther away the parent is from the recipient of the message, the less important the message. Think of the times you have instructed your child to clean up his toys on the floor. If the instructions are shouted from the kitchen into the family room, then the child will most likely not comply. There is no immediate pressure. If, however, the parent walks up to the child and whispers in his ear, "Time to pick up the toys," then the message carries more importance, and the child will most likely cooperate. If you want to be heard and obeyed, then move closer and speak softly.

> **IF YOU WANT TO BE HEARD AND OBEYED, THEN MOVE CLOSER AND SPEAK SOFTLY.**

TALL ORDER

It is easier to enforce kindness in the home than out in the world. There are times our children will be treated unkindly. I (Becky) remember feeling incensed when a child insulted my preschooler's choice of a backpack.

My son had been feeling like a big boy as he went to school with his new backpack.

"That's a baby backpack!" another boy said to him.

My son lowered his eyes and dropped his head. Now, instead of pride, he felt shame. (Poor kid. I saw him shrink a little.)

My mama bear rose to the surface ready for battle. "How could that boy be so cruel? What's wrong with his parents? Didn't they teach him to be kind?"

With difficulty, I managed to keep my mama bear quiet. My son needed help filtering through this more than he needed my righteous anger. We talked about the incident. We discussed how kids and adults sometimes say mean things. We thought about times we had been unkind. (Meanwhile, I still felt pretty angry with "that kid.") I gave my son advice my mom had given me as a child: "What your friend said wasn't nice, but maybe he is having a bad day." Learning not to let someone else's bad mood affect yours is a tall order for child and adult.

My son was able to turn the other cheek and respond with forgiveness and kindness. (It took me a little longer.) "If someone slaps you on one cheek, turn to them the other also" (Luke 6:29a).

PLAYTIME

Intentionally planning time into our day to hang out with our kids is also an act of kindness. We bless our children when we give them the present of our presence. Can you relate to any of the following feelings of these parents?

♥ "I'm having a hard time relating to my children. I'm great with adults, but the kid thing is harder for me."

♥ "I can't wait till my children are older, then I can really have some fun with them."

♥ "I loved the baby stage, but once kids get mobile I get really anxious."

Some adults are more comfortable with babies; others, with older kids. One of the beautiful things about parenting is learning to enjoy each stage. Here's some of my (Lori) straightforward advice: To appreciate your child at any age, get into his world and get over your preference. It's about being with your child; it's not about your comfort. Discover his

60

likes and dislikes. Enter into his imagination and play along. Take the time to read with and to each other, play a board game, laugh. These actions give the parent fresh perspective and renewed appreciation for who God created that child to be. It can be hard to stop working and sit down and build blocks or have a tea party. Even if the activity isn't your thing, do it. The purpose is connection not parental enjoyment. Enjoyment comes following an attitude adjustment. Being involved and demonstrating interest are bridges that continue to be built throughout life. Your reward is the joy on your child's face and the excitement in his voice when he shares his experiences with you. Write "playtime" in your planner. Check it off like you would any other item you've completed. (I love checking things off a list!) Plan time in your day to play.

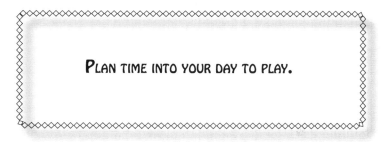

PLAN TIME INTO YOUR DAY TO PLAY.

BEING A FRIEND

Taking time to play with our kids is a great way for kids to learn how to be a good friend. Modeling kind interactions, sharing, taking turns, and being playful gives our children the social tools they need to make and be a friend.

Some children have more trouble with this than others. On a mommy blog, one mom wrote about her child's difficulty making friends. She admitted she didn't know how to help her daughter because friendships were difficult for her, too. I (Lori) was surprised how this struck a chord with so many moms. Lots of mothers commented, saying they too were at a loss because they were unsuccessful themselves. (Here's just a short bunny trail. Let's reach out to each other. Loneliness hurts.)

Both kids who are gifted and kids who have special challenges can have friendship issues. Often they are socially obtuse, not able to pick up on nonverbal messages. These kids need more straightforward instruction. Role-playing is a practical way to encourage the kids who are unable to grasp subtle social skills. The idea of personal space is lost on many kids who struggle socially. Noticing and making inferences about another's feelings is a higher level skill that can be taught. One mom, whose daughter has Asperger syndrome, gets a mirror and teaches her child to make faces. She does this so her little girl is able to show feelings and interpret expressions. Inviting one child over for a playdate and helping with some of the interactions will make the time more pleasant for guest and host. Later, talking about what went well and what things to do differently is a good strategy. With continual encouragement, modeling, and direct training, the child will be better equipped to deal successfully with peers in the neighborhood and at school.

HOMEGROWN

Home is the place where kindness is grown. Demonstrating and expecting kind interactions at home will transfer to kindness outside the home. Becky is good at demonstrating kindness. She takes great interest in people. I've watched her do this with her children and with mine. Being hurried and highly task-oriented gets in the way of kind interactions. I am *so* guilty of that.

So, from one who struggles with slowing down, I'm suggesting doing just that. Kindness is strength in action. Not allowing hurtful interaction draws a clear line between acceptable and unacceptable behavior. When we value kindness in the family, the members feel loved, cared for, and supported. It takes a little more thought and sensitivity to act with tenderness. The fruit that is reaped is sweet: family unity and a child with a caring spirit. First Thessalonians 5:15b advises, "Always try to be kind to each other and to everyone else." Kindness is a choice.

LOVE NOTES ON KINDNESS

LORI WRITES: A friend and I have dubbed each other NSNT and NSNL. NSN stands for "Not so nice." The final letters are the first letters of our first names. We've attempted to help each other *be nicer.* There is no reason why I can't be kind, even when I feel cranky. *Love is kind* is my new mantra.

BECKY WRITES: There are days when Scott and the boys know Mom got up on the wrong side of the bed. A hug usually helps chase my crabbiness away, that and an offer to help with the breakfast dishes! Kindness can conquer the worst of moods.

QUESTIONS

1. How do you encourage kindness in your children?
2. What kind actions could you do for your child?
3. What job could your child do to be of service to the family?

PARENTING TIPS

1. Be direct and specific in communicating; avoid sarcasm.
2. Have your child do or say three kind things after being unkind to a sibling.
3. Take time to play with your child.

PRAYER

Heavenly Father,

Thank You for Your loving-kindness. Help me set a tone of kindness in my family. Let my mouth speak words that are full of tenderness, empathy, and encouragement. Stop me from giving false praise. Let each family member's touches be soft and gentle. Thank You that Your Word teaches my family to help others.

Amen

I AM THE LORD, WHO EXERCISES KINDNESS,
JUSTICE AND RIGHTEOUSNESS ON EARTH,
FOR IN THESE I DELIGHT.

Jeremiah 9:24c-d

SECTION TWO

LOVE IS AN ATTITUDE

Chapter 3

Choose Contentment

Love does not envy.

1 Corinthians 13:4c

I Want...

Not long ago at the grocery store I (Becky) heard a child wail, "I want can-deeee!" The accompanying shrieks assaulted my ears long before I saw the little person responsible for the commotion. Before I had my own kids, I cringed when I heard a child hollering over a toy or treat. I was quite certain when I had kids they wouldn't behave this way. Fast forward a few years, and guess what? I was the mom saying no while my child pitched a fit.

Can't we all relate to this mom? It happens to every parent. A child screeching his demands is normal. He's doing his job, testing the boundaries and declaring his wants. Parents have two choices: give in to the little stinker or hang in there and stay tough. There is a lot more at stake than just getting through the moment. Children cannot have everything their little hearts desire.

Now when I see a parent struggling to stick to his or her guns and say no in the midst of a tantrum, I want to give that parent a high five! That particular day I simply whispered with a smile, "Good for you," as I passed the mom weathering the storm in the store. A high five maybe would have been a little over the top.

An individual's state of contentment is often confirmed by a warm satisfying feeling that all is well. Feeling unsettled usually occurs when expectations aren't met. When our expectations aren't met, envy shows up, leading to jealousy, sibling rivalry, and even theft. We intimately know envy, and most of us would like to tackle that nasty green-eyed monster and toss him right out of our homes. Paul states, "But godliness with contentment is great gain. For we brought nothing into the world, and we take nothing out of it" (1 Timothy 6:6-7). We and our children get caught up striving for things that are temporary and disposable.

Capture Paul's attitude and get ready for action. Awareness of situations that open the door will help prevent Mr. Envy from invading our homes. His goal is to steal happiness and laughter. True contentment with *who* we are and with *what* we have creates joy and satisfaction. These are two emotions worth striving toward and keeping.

Grabby Greed

It is *so* irritating to watch a spoiled, self-centered child. You've seen it: the look of determination with jaw set and eyes gleaming, the arms and hands grabbing, and the legs climbing over others to get whatever is desired. What's worse is the parent who promotes the behavior. This is sometimes done unconsciously and sometimes intentionally. Both Lori and I have had an "aha" moment regarding "the gimmes."

My (Becky) son's sixth birthday party went from festive to fiasco in the blink of an eye. The minute the piñata split and the candy hit the ground, I knew I'd made a *big* mistake. The little guests went wild, scrambling to get to the scattered candy and prizes. The words "That's mine!" and "Gimme that!" filled the back yard. Clunked heads, squashed fingers, and snatched treats added to the pandemonium. The papier-mâché critters seem innocuous, but they can be the catalysts for explosive greediness.

Yep, I've (Lori) had the same experience. But really, what could I expect? The idea is to get the most candy. It's a little kid version of the one with the most toys wins. *Not* a good value to encourage if you're hoping to create an atmosphere of contentment rather than greed.

66

Parents have intentionally encouraged a greedy attitude by saying, "Hurry up. Be first. Get the best. Grab the most." Or they may encourage envy by saying, "How come you're not able to (fill in the blank) like Alison?" Words like this bring discontent into a child's spirit.

Contentment is generally an internal attitude. Kindness and patience are usually observable. Contentment and its opposing trait, envy, are sometimes harder to spot, unless, perhaps, a piñata is involved.

A Desire to Acquire

Society is based on stuff; more stuff, better stuff, now! The more we have, the better we think we feel. Then discontentment creeps in, resulting in envy and more wants. Really, it's simply a case of *gotta have, do, or be more* because someone else has, does, or is more, and we are not happy about it.

Haven't you felt that longing to have what a friend has: the new car, exotic vacation, or a cleaning lady? (I'd *really* like a cleaning lady.) In our desire to have everything the neighbor has, we model envy. This rubs off on our children. What we do with our desire for more determines our degree of contentment with what God has already given us. He knows our envious, hoarding ways and even warns us to be watchful of coveting. "Watch out! Be on your guard against all kinds of greed; a man's life does not consist in the abundance of his possessions" (Luke 12:15).

I tell moms and dads the trick is turning the "I want" into "I can wait" or "I don't need it." Kids don't master this immediately, not even big kids. It takes time and a lot of patience to capture contentment and evict envy.

Toy Store Tactics

Envy shows itself in possessions. For kids, it's their toys. When purchasing gifts for others, the green-eyed monster generally comes out as soon as the child crosses the threshold of the toy store. To halt the monster before it pounces, have a conversation prior to shopping to put positive prevention in play.

Here's an example: "Today we are buying a birthday present for your cousin. (Controller). You get to help pick it out (Chum). You may look at the toys, but I will not buy anything for you today (Coach)." Resist the urge to placate the child by purchasing an additional item for him.

At home, involve your little guy in wrapping the gift. He can make the gift tag and sign his name. As the Consultant, guide the conversation. "What do you think your cousin will say when he opens this package? You chose a great gift!"

Another positive prevention technique Lori and I recommend is a Birthday Wish List, a notebook to keep track of gifts your child likes. To further squelch the "I want" syndrome, use a specific shopping list. Before leaving the house, read over the shopping list. Clearly state the purpose of the errand. "We are going to the store to buy Johnny a birthday gift. We will only be purchasing what's on the list."

At the store, when the child starts in with, "I want," scrutinize the list. Since the item in question is not recorded, simply state, "It's not on the list." This is the perfect time to bring out the Birthday Wish List and add the item while the child watches.

Another toy store tactic is to point out toys the child already has at home. "Look at this cool truck. Don't you have one like that at home? Let's play trucks together when we finish our shopping." Here's a critical point: If you say it, do it.

These techniques begin to address the difference between *need* and *want*. Also the child is reminded of toys he already possesses. The joy of giving to others and contentment are values to encourage.

> ## CONTENTMENT AND THE JOY OF GIVING TO OTHERS ARE VALUES TO ENCOURAGE.

A PLAN AND A PROMISE

Presents and parties can present problems. Gifts and attention given to others can create a stir of envy. There are kids who seem to be content every other day of the year except the day when someone else is being celebrated.

Have you heard or experienced these sentiments?

♥ My six-year-old son has a real problem with his siblings' birthday parties.

♥ My five-year-old daughter has trouble not being the center of attention.

♥ Mother's Day is always difficult at our house.

The above comments occurred in a class focused on setting boundaries. The class members and I (Lori) brainstormed different strategies in dealing with celebration jealousy.

One mom offered a great idea. "I had the same problem with my nine-year-old son," she said. "So I gave him a job and a uniform. He was the party security guard. While wearing his dark official shades, he greeted guests, put the gifts in a pile and collected coats. He felt needed and official." An assignment and a pair of sunglasses solved the problem. I love that idea.

Another way to address party jealousy is to have the child come up with a list of acceptable party behaviors: The child creates The Plan, discusses it with a parent, and promises to follow The Plan. Then both sign The Plan, making it official. If the parent witnesses deviation from The Plan, then the parent calls the child aside. "Please take a break and review The Plan. You can rejoin the party when you are able to keep your promise."

Be proactive and creative when it comes to hosting a party at your home. Plan to stop party envy before it starts.

Attention Surveillance

Parties are not the only events that leave envious children standing in the wings. How does your child feel regarding his peers' achievements? When success isn't being personally enjoyed, it may be difficult to celebrate another's accomplishment. The realization of someone else's goal should give us a happy heart, but at times it doesn't. It's hard to play second fiddle.

Sometimes it's the success of friends, and other times it's the accomplishments of siblings. The harsh reality is that not everyone is good at everything. But everyone is good at *something*. Point out the child's sweet spot. Maybe it's being kind, doing multiplication facts, or running fast.

Few children get the starring role or the blue ribbon. Encourage kids to be content with doing their best and to celebrate the success of others. A final note: This is not easy. To be fair, many of us mature adults struggle with this very issue.

Have a Heart

In our homes we have an opportunity to foster loving and long-lasting relationships between the siblings. Most parents want their children to be friends, not foes. I (Lori) know that is what I hope for my kids. A chasm in any sibling relationship would be very painful.

Let's foster positive interactions between our kids early on. Sibling jealousy doesn't always occur right when child number two enters the family. But rivalry often shows up once the younger child becomes mobile and gets into the older child's space.

When my kids were younger, I'd attempt to give the older child a heart for the younger one. If the younger child got into some of the older child's personal stuff, then I'd say to the older child, "I remember when you were two and you got into my lotion." My purpose was to increase empathy for the younger sibling. By telling a story to the older child about his former escapades, his empathy for the younger one increased. Youngsters love hearing about when they were little.

At my (Becky) house the little brother often wanted to do whatever the big brother did. A helpful tactic was pointing out to the older brother how much the little one wanted to be just like him. "Oh, your little brother sure does think you're special. I've noticed how he tries to be like you."

These small but effective statements set the stage for healthy relationships. Joanne Miller, speaker and author, says she would regularly tell her boys they are each other's best friend. Now as young adults they are.[1]

70

Dump comparisons that foster competition over relationship. Statements like, "Well, your sister never did that!" do not motivate, and they encourage jealousy. By helping the older child filter through frustrating interactions and by avoiding comparisons, parents can support healthy and satisfying sibling relationships.

When we compare, rivalry is birthed and unity destroyed. Just as there is no favoritism with the Lord (Romans 2:11), there should be no favoritism in the home. "It's so much easier for me to connect with one of my twins, not as easy with the other," a dad shared in a class. He was aware of this predicament and chose to be proactive, not to favor one over the other. Recognizing compatibility with one child and not allowing that to turn the other relationship sour was insightful. He chose to exert more effort where needed and continue with the natural connection with the other. Smart dad!

Rivalry may also come in the form of constant arguing. This really gets under a parent's skin! Some sibling squabbles are normal. Home is a place to learn how to disagree without being disagreeable. Lori and I have found parents generally mention the same reasons for friction between siblings: jealousy, competition, boredom, stress, lack of attention, and exhaustion. Parents of young children often need to intervene because little ones don't have the skills to work through issues without guidance. We recommend these steps to help kids disengage from quarreling.

1. Separate siblings.

2. Ask each child to come up with a positive solution to the dispute.

3. Have each child explain the plan he has devised.

4. Encourage compromise, incorporating parts of both plans.

5. Have the kids present their plan to the parent.

6. Allow the kids to come to a final resolution and implement their plan.

Keep a sense of humor. Notice and provide positive feedback when your kids are playing together nicely. Encourage empathy and have an attitude of forgiveness and respectfulness.

Don't play favorites. Pray for positive and supportive relationships to replace rivalry.

> **THE HOME IS A PLACE TO LEARN HOW TO DISAGREE WITHOUT BEING DISAGREEABLE.**

NOT YOURS!

Envy spurs a whole host of negative behaviors. Stealing is one of them. God commands us in the eighth and tenth commandments not to steal or covet (Deuteronomy 5:19, 21). But when an item is *really wanted*, sticky fingers can take over.

Many little children steal. Most don't realize stealing is wrong. Lori and I advocate training kids in the concept of ownership as a precursor for talking about theft. Before a child can understand the meaning of honesty, he needs to comprehend what is his and what is not. Once a child is old enough to grasp the concept of *mine*, usually around two to three years old, it is appropriate to teach respectfulness regarding another's property. In essence, what is *not mine*.

Has a parent ever asked you to borrow a toy at the end of a playdate to avoid a scene when leaving? When this happened to me, I (Lori) was flabbergasted. In my opinion, that was a pretty wimpy way to handle the transition. Parents most comfortable in the Chum role are more likely to use the "borrowing" tactic to keep the peace. Trust us when we say it is better to leave the toy behind and deal with a little fussing than "borrow" the toy to prevent the outburst. A bigger issue is at stake: learning the effects of ownership. As the Controller, set the limits and speak with conviction. "The toy belongs to Kyle and will be here the next time you come to play. When we get home you can play with _____." Then thank the hostess and leave.

72

In my (Lori) experience most children will be fine with this, but some will kick up a fuss. That's okay. The positive piece is the child knows what he wants. (Admittedly, I'm grasping to find the silver lining!) My (Becky) final thought is kids need to learn that not everything belongs to them. Lori and I want to encourage you to be strong and courageous! The transition tantrum is a temporary condition.

Stealing is a tougher situation. The preschool- to school-aged child who possesses the developmental understanding of ownership and takes an item from a friend or retail store needs to make it right. Once the theft is revealed action is needed.

Stealing at this age is usually due to coveting. The child wants the item, so he steals it. I (Lori) tell parents to take the youngster to the scene of the crime. Expect the child to explain what happened, apologize for the behavior, and return the stolen property. If necessary, make amends by requiring the child to pay for the item. Adding to this scenario, I (Becky) would later brainstorm ideas with my child—ways in which he could earn money to pay for things he wants. Ownership that is earned is the message. Include a conversation about how God and your family value and expect honesty. Look at the situation as an opportunity to train your child.

I Did It

Envy is to be squelched but contentment is to be encouraged. Be happy if you do well or if your child does well. God saw His work of creating the universe and all that is in it as good, *really good*. When a child does well, he should feel good. He is one step closer to being internally motivated rather than looking to others for praise.

As one of the younger kids to perform at the piano recital, my (Becky) eight-year-old son was excited and nervous. He had only been taking lessons for a few months as opposed to many of the other seasoned students. His teacher had chosen a simple song for him. The high school students had complex classical pieces listed in the program.

I held my breath when he walked on stage. In his pint-sized suit, he confidently projected his voice and introduced himself, the piece, and composer. Just like a pro, he walked to the piano, adjusted the bench, sat down, took a deep breath, and began to play. I could see his lips moving as he counted each beat. At the conclusion of his performance, he stood tall; took a long, deep bow; and smiled from ear to ear. Tears welled up in my eyes. My son was proud of his accomplishment and so were his dad and I. It was good. No, it was *great*! No one clapped harder than me. Well, maybe his dad!

Parents can encourage their child's feeling of satisfaction by directly rooting for them or indirectly bragging about them. Grandma and Grandpa are the best audience. Here's a warning: Don't use the boasting technique with a parent of a similarly aged child. It won't be appreciated. As you speak to Grandma or Grandpa, your little one may not appear to be listening but will soak in every bit of that conversation. His desire to continue to give his best effort will be reinforced.

Joy Full

What makes your child joyful? When my boys were little the answer would have been, "Cookies!" They loved being welcomed by the smell of chocolate chip cookies after trekking home from school in the snow. Indulging in their favorite sweet put a satisfied grin on each one's face.

What makes you happy? When I asked Lori, she responded, "Walking barefoot on the beach, hiking with Tom and Murphy (her dog), and listening to my kids laugh." For me, my happiest moments revolve around my family, the great outdoors, and of course, a full cookie jar. When your joy-filled moments occur, share your happiness and contentment. Kids want to see their parents happy and visa-versa. Foster a joyful spirit in your child by discovering what makes him smile inside and out.

> **WHEN YOUR JOY-FILLED MOMENTS OCCUR, SHARE YOUR HAPPINESS AND CONTENTMENT.**

To Your Heart's Content

"The happiest people don't have the best of everything; they just make the best of everything they have." This anonymous quote sums up what most parents hope to instill in their children, the virtue of contentment.

Younger kids are good at making the best of what they have. I (Becky) remember planning a day at the children's museum. We were even going to have lunch at a restaurant where the servers wore roller skates! I'd organized it all, but not the blizzard. I was totally bummed; my kids were fine! Both of them were happy to stay home, play Thomas the Tank Engine, and eat mac 'n' cheese from a box for lunch. Once the disappointment wore off, I felt peaceful too. Thankfulness changed my attitude. I had a warm place to be on a snowy day and two little boys who were happy with Thomas, Percy, and James. Although our exciting plans changed, life was good. My heart felt warm. The three of us shared that quiet feeling of contentment. Contentment springs from a grateful heart.

Keep your own heart content by being thankful always. Gratitude is the quality that gives the green-eyed monster the boot. Modeling happiness derived from the satisfaction of a job well done gives kids permission to celebrate doing their best. Count your blessings. Being thankful will create a heart that overflows with gratefulness.

LOVE NOTES ON CONTENTMENT

LORI WRITES: I recall feeling envious of parents who were having success with potty training. It may sound a bit silly, but I actually felt shame and embarrassment over our lack of potty progress. I've come to realize other parents struggle with this same feeling over the same issue. This has taught me to be sensitive and avoid competitively comparing kids. It only causes pain and discontent in others.

BECKY WRITES: Home decorating magazines stir up discontentment in me. If I can take an idea and use what I have to create a new look, great; otherwise, the recipient of the catalog is the recycle bin.

QUESTIONS

1. How do you handle birthday party jealousy?

2. How do you encourage honesty?

3. How would you characterize your children's relationships?

4. What do you do to promote relationship rather than rivalry?

Parenting Tips

1. Promote sibling relationships by avoiding comparisons.

2. Within your child's earshot, brag about his effort and success to Grandma and Grandpa.

3. Discover what brings joy to your child.

Prayer

Father God,

Thank You for the many gifts You have so graciously given my family and me. Your care for us is overwhelmingly good. Please forgive my lust for more. Replace my desire to acquire with a heart of gratitude. Assist me in teaching my children to be thankful. Give us the hearts to cheer one another on. Help me to encourage healthy relationships rather than rivalry. Bring even the small blessings to my attention so I see Your hand in all I do.

In your glorious name I pray,

Amen

BE CONTENT WITH WHAT YOU HAVE.
Hebrews 13:5b

CHAPTER 4

CHOOSE HUMILITY

LOVE ... DOES NOT BOAST, IT IS NOT PROUD.

1 Corinthians 13:4

LOOK AT ME

The whole psychology of self-esteem is out of whack. Lori and I have noticed parents are fearful of injuring their child's psyche so they preach perfection propaganda. They encourage the already egocentric child to believe he's nothing short of perfect.

The funny thing is once kids hit first grade, the gig is up. They know where they stand in comparison to classmates. They know who can read and who may be struggling. It's impossible to be the best and the greatest at everything. We want our kids to have a healthy, proper view of their value, worth, and accomplishments—not an inflated perspective.

I (Becky) loved when my kids were little and they invited me to be their audience. My boys would show off a newly mastered skill and want me to join in their celebration. I recall my oldest son learning how to ride his bike.

"Mommy, watch me!" he called out as he peddled slowly around the driveway on his bike. Wobbling from side to side, he pulled up to me.

"Did you see me? I did it without training wheels, just like a big kid!" He was proud as a peacock.

My joy matched his. "Awesome! Way to go!"

There's a distinction between "Wow! I did it," and "Wow! I am the best." Where does the shift occur between joyful satisfaction and prideful boasting in ourselves and in our kids? How do we maintain an enthusiastic attitude without encouraging a prideful spirit? Just like envy, pride begins with comparisons. While envy thinks someone else has it better, pride believes *I am* better. Pride thrives on other people noticing accomplishment or attractiveness. Its goal is to foster envy in another. This results in the prideful person feeling as if he has elevated his own status. It's the Dr. Seuss' Yertle the Turtle syndrome, stepping on someone in order to step up.

Paul cautions, "Do not think of yourself more highly than you ought, but rather think of yourself with sober judgment" (Romans 12:3b-c). The opposite of pride is humility, sincerely believing all are valuable in God's kingdom. Its attitude is, "We're all in this together." Credit is honestly given or deflected to others. Parent with the goal of giving your child a realistic view of himself and help him see how he fits into the world. Humility glorifies God while pride glorifies self.

> **PARENT WITH THE GOAL TO GIVE YOUR CHILD A REALISTIC VIEW OF HIMSELF AND HOW HE FITS INTO THE WORLD.**

I'M ALL THAT!

Success feels good. A healthy work ethic, putting your best foot forward, and accomplishing a difficult task are positive things. The self-focused part of success is offensive to many people and to God.

In 2 Chronicles 26, the story of King Uzziah is told. The king did "what was right in the eyes of the Lord" and sought God, which led to a successful fifty-two-year reign. God blessed his faithfulness with success in military conquests, agricultural endeavors, and building projects. Unfortunately, pride got in the way. "But after Uzziah became powerful, his pride led to his downfall" (2 Chronicles 26:16a). When eighty courageous priests confronted him with his sin, he became angry. God afflicted him with leprosy. He lost everything—position, health, and the privilege of worshipping in the temple.

His fall is similar to many we see today. When trusted friends identify sin, the prideful response is to discount the observation or to become enraged. We want commendations not criticism. In contrast, the humble heart is grateful for the correction, honesty, and courage friends show. "Pride only breeds quarrels, but wisdom is found in those who take advice" (Proverbs 13:10). A wise person listens and considers loyal advisors and friends' counsel.

The Missing Link

I (Lori) was eight years into my teaching career and married for six before I held my first baby. Prior to that moment I had studied countless how-to books on child rearing. Being an elementary teacher, I was thoroughly trained in child development and discipline. Most of my friends were a few stages ahead of me and were potty training their second child. During my child's first year, I received lots of unsolicited advice. I'd politely smile and disregard every well-meaning word.

"Doesn't she think I know what to do?" I'd lament.

Two years later my second child was born. By this time I was more confident in my role as a mom and ready to receive advice.

Pride is often the manifestation of insecurity. Humility happens when an individual has confidence in a God-given position. When we are humble, we are able to seek, listen to, and consider advice or correction. Instead of being offended, we welcome the input so improvement can be made.

If you notice your child stubbornly ignoring suggestions, making excuses, or arguing over minor corrections, then it would be wise to pray for his self-worth to develop. Find ways for him to participate in confidence-boosting activities. The missing link to humility is self-worth.

Improvement Needed

Correction makes us better. There is no shame in needing improvement. There are even some awards for "Most Improved." Being real with our kids about where they excel and where they need to improve is healthy.

One little girl overheard her gymnastics coach assessing her ability. He was speaking to her mom.

"Well, she's at the bottom of the rung in this class, but she has the heart."

"Is it too much for her? Should we move her down a level?" the mom asked. "Maybe it would be better to be at the top of the heap rather than the bottom."

"Not now. Let's see how she does."

Hearing that more effort was going to be needed, the child worked hard to keep up with the other gymnasts. She listened to the coach's advice and attempted to put it into action. When she received a compliment from this coach, she knew he meant it.

"An aerial like that is worth its weight in gold. The judges will love it. Good job!" Those words were music to her ears.

Although she never quite caught up to the others, her skills improved dramatically. Don't be afraid to correct your child. He can't possibly do everything well. Correction plus encouragement is a great combo.

Humble Hearts

Pride needs other people with which to compare itself. Pride is fostered when others are adequately impressed. It also grows when the prideful person attempts to humiliate another in order to feel good about himself. This is why I'd (Becky) choose a humble friend over a boastful one every day. Why? I can be myself. I don't get caught up in trying to keep up. I don't feel jealous about what I'm missing out on, and I'm not discouraged.

Humility draws people together. Pride divides. One mom gave this account: "I recall waiting for my turn at conferences, getting ready to go into the classroom to speak with a teacher regarding my child's progress and her learning disabilities. Often conferences were hard.

"One incident was especially hurtful. I stood up to enter the classroom as one mom departed. She looked at me (she knew my child

80

struggled) and said, 'Practically perfect.,' waving the report card and pointing to her child. I was happy for both of them; her child had a successful quarter. I felt a twinge of pain in my heart knowing academics were a huge challenge for my child."

Celebrating with each other and recognizing success is good. Let's not take away from the good things others can do. On the flip side, give a large dose of sensitivity to those who may not be in the same boat. Encourage your children to be thoughtful in how they speak about personal accomplishments with other kids who may be struggling. Sharing the results of hurtful pride with our kids will help them distinguish between boasting and confident self-worth.

Prideful behavior is not of God. "For everything in the world—the cravings of sinful man, the lust of his eyes and the boasting of what he has and does—comes not from the Father but from the world" (1 John 2:16). It's easy to recognize the absence of humility in others but a little less simple to see it in ourselves. Rewards will come from earthly accolades or heavenly applause.

Say It Again

"I live with Eeyore," a mom confided. Her child looked at his accomplishments as not quite good enough. She felt she was constantly in the position of propping up her child's view of himself with compliments and praises.

Continually needing to be encouraged or affirmed is not humility; it's low self-esteem. Low self-esteem focuses on self just as much as someone who has an inflated opinion of self. "I can't do that" or "I'm not smart enough" are typical phrases you may hear from a child with a negative self-image. Altering this attitude is not an easy task, but it can be done.

In the situation mentioned above, the mom began to approach her son's negativity as a Coach rather than the Chum. Where the Chum continued to be a cheerleader, the Coach encouraged and redirected. "I really like the way you designed the poster for your book project. How did you come up with that idea?" When the child began reverting back to the negative self-talk, the mother removed herself from the situation. (Sometimes that type of talk is attention-seeking or just habitual.)

Usually a young child that has this view has experienced a lot of defeat, real or imagined. He may have a sibling close in age or a twin who appears to have the world by the tail. This child needs to foster his own interests, separate from his brother or sister. One family has a set of twins where the girls have opposite temperaments. One is positive, outgoing, and generally has a happier outlook. The other child tends to be more negative. The parents have been wise to look for places where the struggling twin experiences success, apart from her sister. They have chosen not to provide extra attention when the child moves into negative self-talk. Instead, they say, "We are all valuable to God, and we are all created in His image." The problem isn't completely resolved, but it occurs less frequently.

Focusing on what the child does well will grow his self-worth. Even the small things like the ability to ties shoes, read a story to a younger sibling, or take out the trash are noteworthy. When children feel confident in the small things, they are more willing to attempt a new task.

> **LOW SELF-ESTEEM FOCUSES ON SELF JUST AS MUCH AS SOMEONE WHO HAS AN INFLATED OPINION OF SELF.**

HOW EMBARRASSING

Embarrassing moments hit us right where it hurts, in our pride. Being a parent really keeps you humble. One Saturday before Christmas, Tom and I (Lori) were taking the kids shopping. Big mistake! Full parking lot, jam-packed aisles, long lines, and cranky shoppers. Tom and I each had two kids in our carts and were weaving through the crowd when our four-year-old's voice rang loud and clear, "Daddy, do you still have diarrhea?"

Heads turned. I bit my cheek to withhold a laugh. My poor husband was beet red! (I still think this is pretty funny.)

My (Becky) most embarrassing moment with one of my boys occurred in the post office. While waiting in line, my son suddenly started hollering at the top of his lungs, "You're not my mommy!" (His preschool teacher had just taught the students a few stranger-danger safety techniques.) People turned and stared. The more I shushed him, the louder he yelled. Sweat was running down my back.

An older woman approached us and said she was about to get the manager, "But in looking at him, he has to be yours. He sure is having fun."

Fun? Yes, at my expense! Now my son and I both laugh when remembering that day. (Ironically, I had just spent that morning helping parents deal with their children's challenging behaviors.)

Both of these stories have been told in our parenting classes. Many moms and dads relate similar experiences. Kids say the darnedest things at the least opportune times. I (Lori) try to console the parents by saying, "It all evens out. When our kids are little, they embarrass us. But when they become teens, we embarrass them." Having a sense of humor over the crazy things kids say and do is the only way to get through some humbling situations.

Let's Play

A parent *can* go overboard with encouragement. I (Becky) made a big mistake when my son was little. I let him win every game. When he'd win, his eyes would dance, he'd clap his chubby little hands, and then pump his arms in the air. So cute! But his reaction was not so cute when he'd play with a more competitive opponent. When he'd lose, his eyes would fill with tears and he'd act out in frustration. I was responsible for his unrealistic expectation of always winning. Ugh!

Competition can be serious business. A person's character is shown in how he acts in competitive situations. We can start teaching good sportsmanship at an early age. This can be done by congratulating the winner of a board game and showing how to lose with self-control and grace. (I had to start over with my little guy!) I taught him to verbalize his feelings by asking him to say, "I tried my best to beat you, but you played better. Congratulations."

A winner of a game could say, "You were a challenging opponent. Thanks for the game." Avoid making excuses or blaming someone or something else for your loss. Teach your children to do the same. Following a sporting event, rather than discussing a referee's poor calls, talk about what each team did well and what both teams can learn from the game.

Many of us have witnessed parents at our children's athletic events screaming obscenities and mocking the officials. I was flabbergasted when Lori told me how she and Tom saw a father attempt to punch an official during their nine-year-old son's football game. Crazy! Some claim that such behavior is part of the game. This type of condoning attitude is typical of our culture. It shows a lack of respect for the person in authority. What are we modeling to our kids? Bad calls are made on and off the field. How we respond tells a lot about our character.

> **BAD CALLS ARE MADE ON AND OFF THE FIELD.
> HOW WE RESPOND TELLS A LOT ABOUT OUR CHARACTER.**

THE SPOTLIGHT

Competitive venues are places where good sportsmanship shines. A good sport has a team mentality. "Be devoted to one another in brotherly love. Honor one another above yourselves" (Romans 12:10). A team player shares the spotlight and spreads the credit for success. Teams rarely win due to one star player. Most victories are the result of teamwork, each individual working with the other individuals toward a common purpose, each player doing his job to the best of his ability. We can apply a team theme to our families.

"Wow! The family-room looks great, Honey," Dad says to Mom.

"Thanks! We worked together. Riley dusted, Blake picked up the toys, and I vacuumed."

"Way to go, Team Anderson! You each did your part and the family room looks terrific."

Train your children to share credit in order to bring graciousness, cohesiveness, and humility into the home.

ON-THE-JOB TRAINING

A humble heart sees the needs of others and quietly steps in to assist. Sometimes people resist lending a hand, thinking they may not be qualified. Giving our kids experience and on-the-job training helps them feel comfortable and confident in serving others. Service can become part of the fabric of family life.

One of the organizations my (Becky) family enjoys supporting is Feed My Starving Children. We pack food packets containing a nutritious rice-based meal that are sent all over the world to feed the hungry. I love when my family volunteers together. Even little ones can help. We line up, assembly-line style. From each station, we can hear the chants of "Chicken, veggies, soy, and rice" as the ingredients are poured into plastic bags, sealed, and boxed. At the end of each shift, leaders pray over the towers of boxes, requesting God's blessing on the shipping and on the recipients of the meals. This has been a great hands-on activity for our family.

Many opportunities exist for family service projects: helping at local food shelves, volunteering at Operation Christmas Child, assisting elderly neighbors with raking leaves, the list goes on. Here's my challenge for you: Find a place for your family to serve together. You will be blessed. Guaranteed!

GIVING OUR KIDS EXPERIENCE AND ON-THE-JOB
TRAINING HELPS THEM FEEL COMFORTABLE
AND CONFIDENT IN SERVING OTHERS.

Lighten Up

Being a parent is serious business. True. But when we take our position too seriously, we forget to have fun. Remember the first time your child laughed? There is nothing better than when you hear your little guy doing a big ol' belly laugh. We love to laugh, and we love making our kids laugh. Sharing a good chuckle bonds family members.

Our blunders and our kids' *faux pas* are not the end of the world. Raising children in a light-hearted environment will promote a good sense of humor. Being able to be a little silly with your children makes home life fun. It's the Chum at his best! So don't be too proud to have a good laugh at your own expense! Laughter is the light side of humility.

Humility is demonstrated in both attitude and action. Thinking of another, sharing credit, serving someone, having a proper perspective of yourself and a good sense of humor are all components of humility. Humility, the antidote to pride.

Love Notes on Humility

LORI WRITES: My four kids attended a book release party held at a local church for Becky's and my first book, *Empowered Parents: Putting Faith First*. As I was signing books, I was distracted by the commotion occurring in the hallway. I looked up and was surprised to see my son and his pal in the corridor enthusiastically jousting with empty plastic liter bottles. I felt a little heat in my cheeks. I was worried what people might think about the sword fight. The play was innocent. It wasn't hurting anyone or even causing a distraction (except to me). Why was this mildly embarrassing? Pride. I was humbled by God's gentle reminder that He's the one I need to look to for affirmation.

BECKY WRITES: A number of years ago I was in charge of a Vacation Bible School at my church. I wrote the curriculum and recruited the teachers. I single-handedly purchased, organized, and delivered the classroom supplies each morning. Others offered to help, but I declined their offers. Although I was exhausted by the end of the week, my pride was fueled from all the compliments. Later a close friend asked me, "Did you need to do this all by yourself? Delegating gives others the opportunity to serve and share in the success." At first, I was really irritated. Then I realized she was right. My pride prevented me from sharing the work and credit.

QUESTIONS:

1. When have you felt hurt by another parent's insensitivity? When have you possibly hurt another parent?
2. How would you describe your child's view of himself? Too high? Too low?
3. How do you encourage a team spirit at home?

PARENTING TIPS

1. Train your child how to lose or win with grace.
2. Provide honest and realistic feedback to your child.
3. Share a good laugh with your child.

PRAYER

Lord Jesus,

You came to us as a baby and a humble servant. Thank You for Your example. Place in me a humble heart. Give me the strength to push pride aside. Move me to give You the glory for any accomplishment so others may be pointed to You. While serving "the least of these" alongside my family members, instill in us a sense of duty and honor. We know when we care for those in need, we are serving You. I long to hear You say, "Well done, my good and faithful servant."

In Your name I pray,

Amen

HUMILITY COMES BEFORE HONOR.
Proverbs 15:33b

SECTION THREE

LOVE IS AN OUTWARD FOCUS

CHAPTER 5

CHOOSE RESPECT

LOVE IS NOT RUDE.

1 Corinthians 13:5a

HUH?

"What is your biggest frustration as a parent?" I (Lori) asked my Facebook friends. The responses I received mirrored what Becky and I have found in our classes. Parents overwhelmingly said, "Listening," or "Selective hearing." Then the complaint is usually followed by this: "My child doesn't do what I tell him to do," or "My child ignores what I say."

This parental exasperation triggered a memory. When I was a child, I was a part of a neighborhood group of seven kids. One boy had an especially free spirit. Since his family ate dinner earlier than the rest of the kids' families, he was never too anxious to leave for dinner while all his pals were still out playing.

"Jimmy, it's time for dinner," his mom's singsong voice would beckon. Fifteen minutes would elapse, and then she would summon him again.

"Time for dinner, Jimmy!" Frustration was evident in her tone. She would hail Jim at least one more time. He would respond with the same lack of compliance.

Then a single-syllabic directive, "Jim!" spoken by a voice a couple octaves lower than the earlier voice, would cause him to run home at top speed. Apparently Jim's dad meant business and Jim knew it. He treated his dad's call as a command and his mom's words more like suggestions.

When parents say *listening* is the main issue at home, what they mean is they are challenged by their child's lack of cooperation and obedience. Translation: The main issue is lack of respect.

Disrespect or rudeness can come in other forms, too: using poor manners, whining, grumbling, sticking out a tongue, and making poor word choices. Becky and I have been working with kids and parents for more than twenty-five years. We've observed a huge shift in respect for authority. In order to have a home where respect reigns, we have to extinguish bad habits, retraining our children and ourselves. It is up to the parents to train children to be respectful. "Honor your father and mother" (Ephesians 6:2a).

SAY IT ONCE

No one likes to repeat themselves. Moms and dads alike feel angry when they have to repeat a directive over and over. It's as if the words disappear into thin air. Some will resort to counting. "One, one and a half, two, two and a half...." Others may yell.

Since those tactics never work well, let's change the mode of delivery to ensure cooperation. Here is Becky's and my bold declaration: Give the statement once. That's right. Once.

"You don't know *my* kid," you say.

Our reply, "We know kids." We also know parents. Like the kids, parents sometimes take the path of least resistance and don't follow through. If you're serious about wanting your little angels to "listen," then you need to get into the game.

Remember the example of Jimmy being called for dinner? What if the scene played out like this: "Jimmy, come home now!" This statement is clear, not confusing. Jim is to go home and to do it now. Then what if the mother stands in the doorway waiting for her son to make his way home? If she sees no movement on her son's part, then she walks out the door toward him. Whoa! Yes, she moves. This always captures a little guy's attention and will most likely cause him to stop what he's doing and return

90

home. If not, then she continues to walk until she is right next to him. He thinks, "I wonder what Mom is up to."

"Home! Now!" Two words delivered quietly in close proximity will most often bring about cooperation.

If a behavioral expectation is stated like a question, "Come home, *okay?*" the child will have the option not to comply. Why would he? A question has been asked and now the little stinker is in the driver's seat. Some parents add an element of pleading to the question, "Come home, please, *pleeeeease.*" Or wheeling and dealing may occur, "If you come now, you can have two slices of cake for dessert." If obedience is desired, don't ask a question, don't whine, or don't bargain. Issue a statement and be ready to move.

Becky and I believe the practice of counting is usually a bad idea. It's human nature to wait for the last number, since that number is the important one. In our Empowered Parent or 1 Corinthians 13 Parent classes, parents of kids with Asperger's or mild autism have said the counting technique is effective. If it works, then use it.

Here are the guidelines to follow if you choose to count. Use a fast *1, 2, 3.* (None of that extended and lingering counting while waiting for the child to cooperate.) Then, as stated above, get into the act. Follow through with whatever consequences may have been stated.

Disrespect with a younger child is more likely to be an issue when the parent falls heavily into the Chum category of parenting. Resentment creeps into the parent-child relationship if the parent is unwilling to be the family leader. The Chum is more apt to back down or make excuses if the child doesn't obey, rationalizing, saying, "I asked him to put his toys away but he's too tired. He missed his nap." If the Controller experiences disrespect, he deals with it immediately. As the Controller, give directives regarding expected behavior. Respect is a necessary virtue for all families.

> **WORDS DELIVERED QUIETLY IN CLOSE PROXIMITY WILL MOST OFTEN BRING ABOUT COOPERATION.**

TRAIN, RETRAIN

Parents are the ones to instill values and train kids in socially acceptable behaviors. This takes time and effort. Kids don't have the depth of experience to know how to act. Little guys typically want to please, so don't assume they are purposely being naughty. Most kids will guess wrong regarding appropriate actions, if left to their own devices. So verbalize and be specific with your expectations.

Some little ones will test the limits if experience has taught them Mom and Dad are not true to their word. Follow through is critical in respect training.

Here is a series of simple steps to gain cooperation, decreasing the challenging moments.

1. State expectations prior to an event. This is positive prevention.
   "Hang onto the cart when we are in the grocery store."
   (Controller)

2. Train while the event is occurring and mention the family value to be reinforced.
   "Remember, hang onto the cart while we are in the store so we can stick together." (Controller/Coach)

3. Retrain with a stated consequence if the child isn't obeying.
   "Hang on or you'll have to get in the cart. To be safe we stick together." (Controller)

4. Follow through with the stated consequence if the child doesn't follow the instruction.
   "In the cart you go. This will keep you safe."
   (Controller)

5. Punishment is the final step. Parent's choice. Try to make it fit the crime. It could look like this:

    "Because it took extra time at the store, when we get home you will have less time to play (or watch a favorite TV show) and more time to think about how you will behave the next time you are in the store with me."

    Note: This punishment still includes training. Have the child take a break to think about what happened and how he will behave in the future and why. When he can tell you this (the younger ones will need help), the time is up (Controller/Coach).

When these steps are taken, the child believes the parent means what he says. After a few episodes like this, he will be more inclined to obey.

MUMBLE GRUMBLE

What happens when a child does what he's been told but grumbles about it? A grumbler mumbles about displeasure. It's his way of indirectly delivering a message of irritation. The mumble-grumble doesn't solve anything. A cranky attitude is one that can change.

In one of my parenting classes, a mother of two shared a frustration. Her school-aged son would grumble while doing a task his mom had given him. This hit the mom's hot button. She would get angry, yet the grumbling only increased. She was at her wits end. I (Lori) asked her if her son completed each task assigned.

She said, "Yes, he does his work, completing what I tell him to do, but he grumbles." This was the positive piece to the puzzle. The child was obeying—not defiant, just crabby. He was doing the job in spite of not wanting to do it. I asked her if she enjoyed every job given to her. She said, "No." Grumbling is an inappropriate expression of displeasure. Together, we worked through some strategies to help both mom and son.

The following techniques are helpful parental actions if you have a grumbler in your home.

1. Teach the child how to express displeasure in a respectful manner (Controller/Coach).

2. Show appreciation when a dreaded task is done (Coach/Chum).

3. Teach the child strategies to make the job more enjoyable, for instance, singing while cleaning or making a list of chores and checking off completed tasks (Coach).

4. Ignore grumbling, but praise good attitudes (Chum).

5. Don't allow the child's mood to control the parent's mood (Controller).

6. Respond rather than react to the situation, saying, "I can see you're unhappy with the job. I appreciate your willingness to do it anyway" (Chum/Coach).

7. Give the child some control. "Empty the garbage sometime before dinner" (Coach/ Controller).

8. Redirect if possible. Have a sense of humor about the bad attitude, without making fun of the child (Chum).

9. Maintain an ongoing attitude that family members work together (Coach).

A lot of grumbling happens at my (Becky) house when my family is overscheduled or overtired.

The saying "It's not your aptitude but your attitude that determines your altitude" was written on a plaque at my (Becky) grandmother's house. She lived to be almost 102 years old with that positive outlook. Unbelievably, I never once heard her complain. A good attitude is a choice. "The cheerful heart has a continual feast" (Proverbs 15:15b).

> ## DON'T ALLOW THE CHILD'S MOOD TO CONTROL THE PARENT'S MOOD.

THE WHINER

Words display attitude and are used to control people. Many parents ask, "Why does my child whine?"

Becky and I will tell you why: "Whining works."

The way to extinguish the whine is to take away its power. Typically, we increase the power of the whine by ignoring it but then, after a few minutes of the irritating sound, we give in to it. In doing this we've taught our children the skill of persistence as it relates to whining.

Whining s-l-o-w-l-y seeps into the home. (I've experienced this.) The whiner uses the behavior to get what he wants and to control the parent. To stop the whining pattern the parent must be willing to see the approach through from beginning to end. I (Lori) had a situation in my home where whining occurred every morning over a hairstyle. Each morning I'd put a ponytail in my third-grade daughter's hair. Every time the style had unwanted bumps. The black holder would be pulled out and I'd try again to reach ponytail perfection. This scene could go on for a long time. I was even beginning to wake up with a stomachache, dreading the morning hair dilemma. The realization hit me, "This is a big problem."

I discussed a new strategy with Tom. My plan was to put on my Controller hat and state to my child, "I'll do your ponytail only two times. If you don't like the first one, I'll be happy to do a second one. Know that you run the risk of the second being worse than the first. The second time's the last time."

The next morning I was ready, armed with my words, "The second time's the last time."

My daughter came into the bathroom for our daily hair ritual. I stated my terms and I delivered my line, "Second time's the last time."

She agreed. Of course, she would. I hadn't given her any reason to believe I'd carry through with this.

I put in the first ponytail.

She ripped out the elastic hair tie.

I restated, "Second time's the last time." She nodded in agreement as I put in the second one.

"It has bumps," she whined. Out it went.

"Second time was the last time," I said.

In a full-blown tantrum she hit the bathroom floor.

I told myself, "Stay cool. Stay strong." I continued to get ready for the day, maneuvering around the flailing body on the tile.

When we got into the car, my youngest child's hair was in disarray. Her face was red and blotchy. Then I looked in the rearview mirror and witnessed the sweetest moment. The older sister was fixing the younger sister's hair. I did not put a stop to it. The second-time's-the-last-time contract was between my youngest child and me. The older sister wasn't a part of the agreement.

The next morning my daughter came into the bathroom with her brush and black elastic holder. The familiar pain returned.

"I know," she said, "second time's the last time." We were off to a good start.

Whining is harder to address away from home. Kids instinctively know adults don't want a scene in public, so they use the most opportune time to create a fuss. Pretty smart! Often fussing happens at the store. As stated in chapter 3, be proactive by making a shopping list and sticking to it. Another helpful tool is to have a statement something like this reserved for whining: "I will listen when you speak respectfully." Or maybe, "My ears pay attention when you speak respectfully." Or simply, "Whining doesn't work." (In one class, I [Lori] recommended saying, "My ears can't

96

hear whining." One mom used this technique and reported the results to the class the following week. Her little whippersnapper retorted, "Mom, that's a lie." I don't promote using that line anymore.)

Usually around the age of eight or nine a child begins to have strong opinions. He will often state his thoughts and stubbornly refuse to change his mind. Rather than standing firm after delivering a solid no, the parent begins to back off and give in. This is why whining is so insidious and prevalent at the middle elementary age. To extinguish whining, have a plan. Stand firm.

> ## To extinguish whining, have a plan. Stand firm.

Elementary Etiquette

Being able to communicate by using good manners demonstrates respect. Society doesn't expect, and sometimes rejects, polite behavior. Look at the myriad of television shows that are crass and disrespectful. Yet, who do you want to hang out with, civil people or rude folks?

A parent survey was done to determine topics of most interest for an ongoing parenting class that Becky teaches. The overwhelming top choice for parents was manners. Part of a good parenting plan is etiquette. When teaching manners, start when the kids are young. Even little ones are capable of using "please" and "thank you." Other than saying please and thank you, it is best to teach good table manners at a time separate from the actual mealtime. Meals are about coming together, enjoying each other's company. Keep them as stress-free as possible.

(Becky and I agree to disagree on this. Here's a little point/counterpoint from your authors: Becky uses mealtime as an opportunity for on-the-job training. I think that is okay only if it isn't the main focus and if it's done in very small doses. If manners become the main meal objective, then indigestion will be the result.)

One way I reinforced good table manners was to have a tea party with my kids. Becky laughs and says this approach wouldn't have worked in her home. Instead, she turned into the "crabby waitress."

Here are a few tips for teaching tea party or restaurant manners using the Controller and Coach techniques:

1. Pray before eating, thanking God for His provision.

2. Get dramatic. Throw in a British accent at the tea party or don an apron and smack some gum as the crabby waitress.

3. Give directives in the positive. Rather than saying, "Don't talk with your mouth full," say, "Please swallow your food before you speak." (The crabby waitress has license to be a little brash. "Hey! Chew with your mouth closed, Mister.")

4. Give children a reason for a particular directive, for example, a napkin in your lap keeps food off your clothing in case you spill.

5. Emphasize sitting at the table until all are finished. Ask to be excused from the table.

6. Use a quiet, inside voice. Involve everyone in the conversation.

Learning to be polite takes time. Avoid embarrassing or shaming the child. Model good manners. Keep reinforcing polite words and actions. If you play and practice table etiquette, then your child's good manners will transfer to meals anywhere. You'll be pleased with the results.

Hurry Up!

Punctuality and timeliness also fall into the politeness category. Dawdling and little people seem to go hand in hand; mealtime can be the worst. Dawdling happens when daydreams or distractions occur. Sometimes, like grumbling, it's a passive-aggressive demonstration of resistance. Whatever the slow poke's motivation the solution is the same. Get an old-fashioned timer. As the Controller, set the timer for the amount of time it ought to take to start and finish a meal. Next, communicate to the child, "When the timer rings, breakfast is done, and then we are leaving."

Don't be tempted to hang around and hurry the child. Say nothing, allowing the child to be in charge. When the timer rings, follow through. "Oh, the timer has rung. We have to go." A protest may ensue. The next parental response demonstrates you are on the child's side, so allow the timer to be the bad guy by saying, "Oh, I wish you had more time to finish, but the timer rang and we have to go." Clear the plates and go. It may feel mean, but resist the urge to haul the leftover food along in the car. Really, your child will be fine.

Clean Up

Eating and cleaning up are two things done a million times throughout the day with little kids. A routine is needed for playtime: (1) Take out item; (2) Play with item; (3) Put item away. Establish a 1-2-3 order for using things to demonstrate respect for property. When toys are left out, clutter increases and there is a greater likelihood they will get stepped on or tripped over. Your little guy will need Mom or Dad's help putting things away. When it is time to pick up, get involved and be specific rather than vague. Say, "I'll put away four things, and you put away four," for example, or "You pick up the puzzle and put it in the box and on the shelf, and I'll put the cars into the plastic container." If you choose not to be involved in the process, your child will be less likely to follow through, thinking you don't mean business. Getting kids into the practice of cleaning up after themselves takes parental enforcement and involvement.

After the 1-2-3 routine, the next event can take place. "After we put the toys away," you might say, "we can have a snack." A child that has learned to put things away before moving onto another activity will be more responsible with possessions and will have learned valuable organizational techniques.

The Raspberries

"Is it a big deal when my child sticks his tongue out at me or gives me the raspberries?" a mom asked.

Yes! It is a *very big* deal. The protruding tongue is the little kid version of a teen's hand gesture. Avoid reacting when you see your child's tongue defiantly aimed in your direction, but *do* respond.

First, train: "Tongues are for talking and eating. Sticking out a tongue is disrespectful. We want respect in our home." Next, retrain: "I see you are *angry* with me." (Name the particular emotion.) "Use your words to tell me what you don't like." Finally, punish: "Go to your room and think about a better way you will act the next time you are angry with me." (Some parents may choose to include a spanking for disrespect. For more information on spanking, see chapter 7.)

It is up to us to help our kids learn what honoring a parent means. They will not show respect or honor unless taught.

Honor Your Parents

God commands us to honor our parents. Modeling is one way to accomplish this. My (Becky) great aunt lived close to us and later in life needed a lot of assistance. Each week, I would shop with her for groceries and take her to appointments. Often I included my sons. My boys would get involved by pushing the grocery cart, hauling bags of food, and opening doors. Aunt Ruthie was entertained with their stories about school, Cub Scouts, and soccer. By observing me serve Ruthie, they learned a lot about how to show honor to another. When kids learn how to be respectful in the family, they will understand what it means to honor God.

Respect God

Being obedient and cooperative shows respect. Our speech communicates respect as well. We show respect to others by the way we speak to them and about them. The same holds true for our respect for God. The third commandment requires respect of His holy name.

When my (Becky) boys were in elementary school, every once in a while one of their visiting friends would shout out an inappropriate word. In order to squelch the unacceptable language, I would immediately show up in the back yard (or wherever they were) with treats and include a quick chat. "We treat God's name with respect at our house," I'd say. I have found this is a constant battle, but speaking family expectations works. The kids' friends always come back!

Listen Up

Patience, kindness, contentment, and humility are components to building a home that embraces respect. When we respect God and others, it is easier to avoid selfishness, sinful anger, unforgiveness, and temptation. If rudeness or disrespect is not dealt with, then those behaviors will only get worse. Expect respect and reinforce respectful behavior in the home. When you do this, you will find your child is a better listener.

Love Notes on Respect

Lori writes: I worked with a teacher who said she never smiled before Thanksgiving so her students would be more likely to obey—a sad method, in my opinion. I believe kids are more likely to obey when they feel love and know the rules. Respect born out of fear brings obedience only when the authority figure is present. Respect generated from a relationship produces obedience even when the authority figure is absent.

Becky writes: It's been really helpful in our family to prep the boys before different social gatherings so they know what is expected. This includes practicing shaking hands, thanking the hosts, and of course, table manners.

Questions

1. How well do your children follow your instructions?
2. What could you do to help your child be more obedient?
3. What disrespectful behavior needs to be addressed in your home? What is your plan?

Parenting Tips

1. Use positive prevention. State expectations.

2. Train children to use good manners.

3. Deal with disrespect immediately.

Prayer

Father, heavenly King,

Convict me when I don't demonstrate respect. Help me to be a good example of a person who respects others and respects You. Give me the strength and vision to deal with disrespectful actions or words from my children. Don't let me fall into the trap of excusing my children's rude behavior. Let my home be one that overflows with respect, honor, and love. Start with me.

Amen

Show proper respect to everyone.
1 Peter 2:17a

Chapter 6

Choose Unselfishness

Love is not self-seeking.

1 Corinthians 13:5b

Superhero!

Did you happen to hear about the dad of two who chased down a would-be kidnapper to save a neighbor girl? I (Lori) was glued to the television when this was reported. So heroic! This man thought nothing of his own safety and didn't care about potential damage to his van. His only thoughts were to save that little girl. He was brave and unselfish.

Here are a few other acts of unselfishness done by family men that haven't made it into the news: the dad who shaved his head before his son's first chemo appointment, the husband who stayed up Mother's Day eve to wallpaper a bathroom for his wife, a man who chose not to open his eye clinic on Saturdays so he could coach his son's football team, the father who spent a day of his much-needed vacation shopping with his girls. All sacrifices in appearance, sleep, finances, time. Everyday heroes.

My (Becky) dad will always be my hero. It seemed as if he knew how to do everything. He shared his love of the outdoors and sports with me. He taught me how to fillet a fish, do a handstand off the diving board, and navigate a double black diamond. He took the time to share his zest for life with me.

Kids need superheroes in their lives. It takes time, effort, and a large helping of unselfishness to be a parent who acts with generosity, empathy, and humility. When we are selfless, we are able to serve each other and see another's point of view. We learn to be less selfish when we become parents. Priorities shift. Like respect, unselfishness is outwardly focused. Young children are highly egocentric. And parents, although less selfish since having a baby, still fight against the sin of it's all about me.

Selfishness, manifested in child or adult, is the quality that's most detrimental to the family. "Do not forget to do good and to share with others, for with such sacrifices God is pleased" (Hebrews 13:16). Superheroes aren't selfish.

> ## SELFISHNESS, MANIFESTED IN CHILD OR ADULT, IS THE QUALITY THAT'S MOST DETRIMENTAL TO THE FAMILY.

New Shoes

Putting ourselves in someone else's shoes is the best way to get a glimpse into what makes him tick and how he may feel. My (Becky) dad quit downhill skiing, one of his favorite sports, for six years. I had been diagnosed with scoliosis. I had to wear a back brace and wasn't permitted to ski. Since I couldn't go, he wouldn't participate either. His empathetic gesture still brings tears to my eyes. "Live in harmony with one another, be sympathetic" (1 Peter 3:8b).

The Golden Rule in Matthew 7:12a states, "So in everything, do to others what you would have them do to you." Combining empathy with respect will change the way we interact with family members. Rather than thinking, *My child's behavior is bugging me,* or *My child is embarrassing me,* look for the deeper reason for the annoyance. Parents want the nasty behavior to go away but often forget to look for a long-term solution. There may be a character trait that needs to be developed or a need that is not being met.

Because "God created mankind in his own image" (Genesis 1:27a), we are rational, volitional, relational, emotional, and spiritual beings. These qualities spur on legitimate needs in every individual. The five needs of respect, freedom, security, fun, and spirituality are best met in the context of a right relationship with God and fellow human beings.

Behavior is driven by needs and is influenced by personality type, developmental stage, gender, and the home environment. The five basic needs are respect, freedom, security, joy, and spiritual fulfillment. Basic human needs must be addressed in a godly way, or an ungodly substitute will result. Below, you will see how being created in God's image naturally generates a specific human need.

God's Image	Human Need Generated
Rational (God is logical, thinking)	Respect
Volitional (God has a will, is powerful, and independent)	Freedom
Relational (God is relational in the Trinity)	Security/Belonging/Love
Emotional (God has emotion)	Joy, Fun
Spiritual (God is spirit)	Spiritual Fulfillment

Understanding our God-image helps us discern why a child may be acting or responding a particular way. Developmentally, little ones have a large need for belonging and security. Even if you want your child to get moving, avoid saying, "If you don't come, I'm going to leave you." Controller types tend to use this comment in transition situations, such as exiting the park or the toy department. This declaration hits right to the heart of a child's need for belonging and security. In Hebrews 13:5, God tells us He will never leave or forsake us. We should model and express that same sentiment. Instead, say, "I will not leave without you. I love you. You can walk to the car by yourself or I will carry you. You choose." Not leaving or forsaking, that's the message to give. (For cooperation techniques, see chapter 7.)

Look at your young one's behavior. Try to analyze it through their needs sieve. Determine what need could be lacking and how that need can be met. Of course, God is the only one who can fully meet all our needs. Here are a few general examples. Specific answers will vary given the circumstances and the child:

Child's Statement (Cue)	Translation	Parental Response
"Do it by self."	"I need respect."	"I think you can. Let me know if I can help."
"No!"	"I need freedom."	"You can choose to do this or that."
"Joey doesn't like me."	"I need to belong."	"I remember when that happened to me." (Fill in your story to create a common bond.)
"Push me on the swing!"	"I need fun!"	"Sure! I love to play with you!"
"Do we eat in heaven?"	"I need to know about God."	"Let's see what the Bible says!"

Watch for words that convey a consistent need. Attempt to provide positive and godly ways to meet those areas that may require extra nourishment. Listen for the clues.

TIME TO EAT

While needs are innate, schedules are somewhat negotiable. Family dinnertime is disappearing from the home. Becky and I both believe this is sad. Shared time around the table is critical for family unity. Becky says, "Having dinner with my family is one of my favorite things. All is well when the four of us have our knees tucked under the kitchen table, sharing stories of the day."

It's true. Dinnertime connects and cements relationships. Realistically, finding time to eat together can be difficult, but it's worth the fight. William Doherty and Barbara Z. Carlson tackle this issue in their book *Putting Family First*. "For reclaiming family meals," they say, "our advice is simple but challenging. Make family meals a priority, be flexible and start from where you are."[2] They suggest keeping a chart of family meals—breakfast, lunch, and dinner—in order to determine how often you actually eat together.

One young mom shared how she was setting the pace for her young family and keeping family meals a sacred time. She put the following message on her voicemail: "If you're calling between the hours of five and six, we will not be answering our phone. We are having family mealtime. Feel free to leave a message and we'll return your call after six." Isn't that awesome? Not answering the phone, not texting, not watching TV, and not using computers or iPads during dinner all send the message, "Family time is special and not to be interrupted." Work to make this time a priority with each family member.

Individual activities plus long hours at the office may impede our spiritual and family life. It's a grind, trying to get ahead or attempting to catch up. It's often unavoidable. But when it's a matter of choice, ask yourself, "What's the cost to my family?" and "Does the schedule reflect my family's values?" Asking these questions may help put work-a-holism and personal endeavors into perspective. "You may say to yourself, 'My power and the strength of my hands have produced this wealth for me.' But remember the LORD your God, for it is he who gives you the ability to produce wealth, and so confirms his covenant, which he swore to your ancestors, as it is today" (Deuteronomy 8:17-18).

PRESSURE COOKER

Busyness isn't only an adult issue. Kids today have a lot going on, and many are experiencing stress from a combination and culmination of things. Academics and extracurricular activities, even if enjoyed by the child, may be catalysts for anxiety. Seasoned principal Kathy Namura has seen the effects of stress on students. "Parents need to praise the child for work well done rather than give the message that the hard work he did wasn't good enough. Expecting too much causes undo stress on children. I've observed stress-related stomachaches and headaches."[3] Academics and schedules are both potential pressure cookers.

A mother of an elementary school child shared her experience:

> My nine-year-old said, "I just want to kill myself."
> I couldn't believe what I was hearing. It cut straight to my heart. As my son sobbed he expressed he was overwhelmed with life.
>
> What an irony; I thought my husband and I were providing everything our child wanted. He was involved in the gifted and accelerated classes at school, taking piano and guitar lessons, playing basketball, and attending Wednesday evening church classes. Academic, creative, physical, and spiritual needs were being addressed. Our son enjoyed all of these things. We hadn't realized we were setting him up for failure by letting him do everything he wanted. He couldn't cope with the pressure of being so busy. He had no time left to play and be a kid. By providing our son with all of these activities, we'd unintentionally set him up to fail. Stress was taking its toll.
>
> This scene still continues to play in my mind's eye. I vividly remember that awful night, sitting with him, holding him, letting him cry, trying to soothe him, and telling him how much he was loved by his dad and me, and by God. I prayed hard that night, asking God to help me help my son. God faithfully gave me the answer. He reminded me for this boy, less is best.
>
> My husband and I, with our son's input, took time to prioritize interests. We identified items that could wait and those that could be eliminated. It took a time to cut back on our commitments and responsibilities, but we were able to do it. The result was life-changing.
>
> We're still careful to not always give our son everything he asks for because we recall the night he was overwhelmed with life. We've learned less usually is best.

In the story above, the mom's bent is highly extraverted; she is energized by being with people. Yet her child's personality is highly introverted; he gains energy when alone. All the action seemed comfortable and natural to the mom. She knew her boy enjoyed each individual activity. It made sense to allow him to experience them. But she and the boy's dad hadn't realized how stressful the combination of obligations was for their child. God sweetly gave her a wake-up call. Her son articulated his need for unstructured time. She and her husband were wise. They listened and adjusted their son's schedule accordingly.

Prioritizing activities and keeping your child's personality in mind will help determine how much involvement in activities outside the home your child can successfully manage.

> ## ACADEMICS AND EXTRACURRICULAR ACTIVITIES, EVEN IF ENJOYED BY THE CHILD, MAY BE CATALYSTS FOR ANXIETY.

IT'S MINE

Families will experience less frustration and stress if they take stock of priorities and understand developmental stages. Through evaluation and knowledge, you can set reasonable expectations. So you ask, "What can a parent expect from a two-year-old when attempting to train him in unselfishness? How does one promote unselfishness with a toddler?" We all know a two-year-old thinks everything belongs to him and he doesn't play well with age-mates. In the toddler's world, it is all about him! Language skills and physical development are moving at lightning speed. The idea of a friendship is just beginning to emerge. Playing alongside rather than *with* another child is what a two-year-old's playdate will look like. The social skill of interacting with a friend while playing emerges closer to age three. If you think your child will be sharing at age two, you are mistaken. I can almost hear some readers breathe a sigh of relief: "Oh, my child isn't a selfish brat; he's just normal."

Before sharing can take place, ownership needs to be comprehended. This is why at two years old everything is "Mine!" Don't let this prevent you from saying, "The keys belong to Daddy." Defining who owns what is appropriate.

A two-year-old does love to help with household chores. This is where you can begin to train your little one in unselfishness. Helping around the house, serving others, and working together results in unselfishness and cooperation, and these are things a two-year-old can do.

Trade Ya

The three-year-old isn't into sharing either. But he is a little more cooperative and agreeable than he was at age two. To introduce the concept of unselfishness, start with the idea of trading. "You can play with the toy for fifteen minutes. Then trade toys with your friend." Set a timer. After trading has been successfully practiced, taking turns is introduced. "When the timer rings, it's Sammy's turn to play with the ball." Three-year-olds have a sustained attention span. They are able to play with items for close to twenty minutes! Typically, between three and a half and four the child will be able to share.

This doesn't mean he has to share everything. He can have some things that are strictly his own. Allow him to choose which toys need to be put away before a friend comes to play. If he has something that is dear to him, keep it away from friends and siblings. Ownership and responsibility are good traits, too. Treasured toys at our (Lori) home remained in the child's room, and toys for all were kept in the family room. Pick a place to store items to be shared, and find a location for those special items that are to be used by only one.

Treasured Gifts

Once a child is able to understand ownership and sharing, giving things away is the next developmental milestone. Giving and receiving are best understood at age six and older.

A mother of two and a reading specialist, Keri Buisman relates how her own child and one of her students impacted her view of demonstrating God's love through generosity:

My students struggle in the area of reading. At the end of each school year I give my pupils a book as a gift with the hope that the children will read over the summer.

I explained the book gifts to my third-grade daughter. An avid reader herself, she thought this was a great idea and wanted to get involved. Immediately she told me I could have all of her Cam Jansen books. This series has been one of her favorites and she frequently rereads the books.

"The books are gifts, so you won't get them back," I said. I suggested only taking a couple, knowing how much she treasured these books.

One of my students also enjoyed the Cam Jansen series. She'd just begun reading the first book of the series and loved it. Since my daughter was on board with this plan, I gave that student the second and third books to take home and keep. She was overjoyed.

She replied, "Now I have five books of my very own at home!"

Five books to call her own; my own child has a bookcase overflowing with books. I was so moved by this. During dinner that evening I told my daughter about the student's reaction to the books. I was excited to share the impact of her generosity on another child. I thought my daughter would feel proud and happy about giving away her books. Instead, she was angry. "You only gave her two?" she said. "I told you to give her the whole series. She could have had so much more!"

My daughter didn't put limits on her love and generosity; she wanted to share it all and not hold anything back. She was willing to give away a treasured collection so another child could be blessed.[4]

"For where your treasure is, there your heart will be also" (Matthew 6:21). Giving our best and most treasured possessions is true generosity. This type of giving comes with a price, personal sacrifice. True sacrifice results in an enormous blessing to both the giver and recipient. Money and material items are tools given to us by God to help others.

> ## GIVING OUR BEST AND MOST TREASURED POSSESSIONS IS TRUE GENEROSITY.

GOOD WILL

Doing household chores, sharing, and giving things away are three good ways to encourage unselfishness. Becky and I came up with some additional ideas to reinforce the concept of graciousness and generosity in little kids.

1. When hosting a playdate at your home, have your child allow the guest to choose first. (There is a potential unfairness factor. The guest philosophy may not be reciprocated.) This idea works best with children five and older.
2. Give him the job of feeding the family pet. (Caring for another lessens selfishness.) This job could even be done by a child as young as two with proper parental assistance.

3. Use his allowance money for the month of December to buy a gift for a needy child. Children six and older will be most interested in carrying through with this plan.

4. Use the Divide 'n' Decide technique. One child splits the last slice of dessert, and the other chooses first.

5. Have the older sibling teach the younger one a new game or skill.

6. Rotate the first choice between the children. Parents never need to keep track. The kids always know whose turn it is to go first.

7. Role-play various situations that will require sharing.

8. Use sharing language. "Sure, I'd be glad to share my _____ with you."

9. Encourage children to contribute to the offering plate at church.

10. When kids receive new toys, encourage them to choose gently used toys to donate to charity.

11. Most parents of little kids know children are geared to be selfish. Home is the best place to instill the value of being charitable and big-hearted.

Selfish Ambitions

The Lord gives many examples of both selfish and unselfish men and women in the Bible. Few stories are as poignant as the tale of Abraham and Lot. The two men had been blessed with numerous flocks, and to avoid conflict between their herdsmen, they decided to separate. Abraham divided the land into two sections and gave his nephew first choice. "Lot looked around and saw that the whole plain of the Jordan toward Zoar was well watered, like the garden of the Lord, like the land of Egypt. (This was before the Lord destroyed Sodom and Gomorrah.) So Lot chose for himself the whole plain of the Jordan and set out toward the east" (Genesis 13:10-11a). Lot chose the best for himself. Unfortunately, the best was in close proximity to the sinful city of Sodom.

People often choose the best for themselves and the consequences are not always good.

Lot's selfish choice was his downfall. In Genesis 13:12, Lot was living near Sodom. By chapter 14, he was living *in* Sodom. Finally, in Genesis 19:1, he was counted among the prominent men of the city. Shortly after that, Sodom was wiped out due to its sinfulness. Lot was saved, but he lost everything, including his wife.

Selfish behavior is destructive. Marriages are mangled, relationships are ruined, and families are fractured. Placing the wants and needs of others before our own is an act of unselfishness. Paul wrote to the Philippians, "Do nothing out of selfish ambition or vain conceit, but in humility consider others better than yourselves. Each of you should look not only to your own interests, but also to the interests of others" (Philippians 2:3-4). This can be modeled daily to our children in the way we treat our spouse and other family members.

ETERNAL EYES

Managing time, money, and possessions with an eternal focus leaves a model of faith and love for our children. Thanking God for His provisions and the opportunity to use your gifts is good modeling. When kids witness this attitude of gratefulness for God's blessings, an appreciation of God begins to emerge, and the spirit of reaching out to someone else is fostered. Unselfish love looks for ways to meet legitimate needs in others. We can support and encourage our kids' efforts to give their time and treasures to meet someone else's needs. Jesus taught in actions and words the importance of humbly serving others when He washed the disciples' feet (John 13:1-17). Service can happen anytime, anywhere, but surrender is needed. Pastor Larry Renoe says, "You'll know if you have a servant's heart by how you'll respond when treated like one."[5]

SERVING OR SELF-SERVING?

What draws your family away from church? Are sports, clubs, or other events consuming your time? A Minnesota pastor bravely took a stand and exclaimed to his congregation, "I hate hockey." Hockey practice was taking families from the pews to the bleachers on Sunday mornings. Hockey isn't the only activity that takes families away from worship. The Bible is clear, "Do not make any idols" (Exodus 34:17). Idols can be possessions, activities, and even people.

School choice, academics, athletics, talents, and relationships can be elevated to an idol standard. Even volunteer work can become an idol. Idols are often good things exaggerated. They won't look detestable and may even provide a sense of comfort. Step back and take a look at your family's priorities. Evaluate your observations. Ask, "Is this in a proper heavenly perspective?"

Anything you and I (Lori) place above our love for the Lord becomes an idol. Okay, here are two convicting questions. (Just so you know, I've asked myself these questions and I'm not pleased with my answers.) Do you bow to the throne of God, or are you sitting on it? Are you your own idol?

Foster God-chasing rather than self-seeking in your relationships and resources. Look for ways to be God's instrument to meet the needs of your children and others. When you do, your children will be blessed by your example.

God jealously desires to have the highest place in our hearts and our kids' hearts. When He reigns first, He will use us to meet the needs of others. Unselfishness will come more naturally. God is jealous for us because putting God first is what is best for everyone.

> EVALUATE WHAT YOU ESTEEM, AND ASK, "IS THIS IN A PROPER HEAVENLY PERSPECTIVE?"

LOVE NOTES ON UNSELFISHNESS

LORI WRITES: I found it really hard when I would encourage my children to share and then visit another family where sharing wasn't expected. That scenario was challenging for both my kids and me. I discovered that talking about differing family values, prior to a playdate, helped when my kids were at least four years of age. As much as I would have liked to, there was nothing I could do to change another family's value system.

BECKY WRITES: As a young mom I would get anxious when other moms asked if my kids were participating in X, Y, and Z. A mom with older kids gave me some great advice. She told me children don't need to experience every activity before they are in kindergarten. Her words gave me permission and confidence to say no to the popular busyness trend. What a relief! The blank days on my calendar are a stress-free gift!

QUESTIONS

1. Identify needs in your children that are not being met. How can you satisfy those needs?

2. How would you describe your family calendar? Does it need to be adjusted? What will you do?

3. How will you foster an attitude of service in your children?

PARENTING TIPS

1. Listen for words that convey a consistent need. Provide and pray for a godly filling.

2. Encourage sharing through trading and taking turns.

3. Allow your child to help with household chores.

PRAYER

Heavenly Father,

You gave Your one and only Son to die for the sins of the world. Only You are completely unselfish. Thank You for Your precious gift of salvation. Please mold me into Your likeness. Help me to extinguish selfish thoughts and actions. I want to act with generosity, empathy, and humility. Give me and my children opportunities to serve others.

In Jesus' name I pray,

Amen

COMMAND THEM TO DO GOOD, TO BE RICH IN GOOD DEEDS, AND TO BE GENEROUS AND WILLING TO SHARE.

1 Timothy 6:18

SECTION FOUR

LOVE IS SELF-CONTROLLED

CHAPTER 7

CHOOSE PEACE

LOVE ... IS NOT EASILY ANGERED.

1 Corinthians 13:5c

ANGER MANAGEMENT

"Don't drag me into your hell!" A young woman's voice pierced the din of the crowd.

Scott, my boys, and I (Becky) turned to see what the commotion was all about. I vividly recall the details of the scene that day. A hush settled over the busy restaurant. A preschooler and his mom were in full tantrum mode.

"You are ruining my day!" the child's mother yelled at the top of her lungs.

Eyes followed the angry duo as the mom scooped up her screaming child and dashed out of the restaurant into the crowded amusement park at warp speed.

Shocking, yes. But to be fair, how many times have we as parents let our anger get the best of us? It occurs more often than we may like to admit.

"I never understood how anyone could abuse a baby or child. Then I had my own son," said one seasoned mother of two who is a teacher with a master's degree in early childhood education. "My son was diagnosed with Asperger's and ADD. My daughter also has attention issues. They are both in college now, but raising them was challenging.

119

Looking back, I have to say I wouldn't want them to be any different." This mother never abused her children, yet she could understand the powerful emotions and frustrating occurrences that surround parenting young children.

Let's face it. We are passionate about and heavily invested in our children. This is most likely why we can have such strong reactions. Responding with wisdom and self-control is always better, but sometimes our anger gets the best of us.

The word *fool* is tied to angry outbursts in Scripture. Here are three examples: "A fool gives full vent to his anger" (Proverbs 29:11a). "A fool shows his annoyance at once" (Proverbs 12:16a). "A fool is hotheaded and reckless" (Proverbs 14:16b).

Anger is a secondary emotion triggered by a primary emotion. Frustration, annoyance, chaos, and a lack of understanding can be catalysts to an ungodly expression of anger. Anger isn't sinful in and of itself; it's a God-given emotion. It's how we choose to express our anger that can be harmful.

We'll examine unleashed anger in both parents and kids. Identifying, interrupting, and initiating a plan for a wise, self-controlled, peaceful response to hot spots is what we want, instead of the knee-jerk reaction of rage. Anger and its antithesis peace are both choices.

Name It

"I'm mad at you." If your child can say these words, pat yourself on the back. He's able to identify his feelings. The basic feelings of mad, glad, or sad are emotions little ones have an ability to name. Once the emotion is identified it is easier to deal with.

Adults who are not self-aware have problems knowing when an outburst is coming. Without warning, *MAD* explodes, getting the whole body into the act: a furrowed brow, pursed lips, waving arms, pointing fingers, stomping feet. Proverbs 15:18 says, "A hot-tempered man stirs up dissention, but a patient man calms a quarrel." To avoid these anger antics it's time to notice the physical changes that occur prior to mad mode.

Little kids can be a bit more creative when mad. I (Lori) had a hair-puller (she pulled out her own hair), a screamer and a tree climber (similar to running away), a granola guy (put granola in my shoe once when told no), and a flailer (the ultimate tantrum).

None of these physical reactions are productive to solving the angry person's problem. Becoming more self-aware allows both child and adult to recognize the anger signs. Ask your child, or yourself, "How do you feel just before you get mad? Does your heart beat faster? Do your hands sweat?" My kids told me that I got the "mad face." Identify the anger warning signals. Being able to state, "I'm beginning to feel angry," is the first step to self-control.

"My dear brothers, take note of this: Everyone should be quick to listen, slow to speak and slow to become angry, for man's anger does not bring about the righteous life that God desires" (James 1:19-20). Just three responses are needed to prevent ungodly anger: Be quick to listen, slow to speak, and slow to become angry. Once in mad mode, it's hard to step back, so be aware of the warning signs.

Stop It

Once anger is felt and identified, how can it be slowed down? Interrupting the feeling flow is the best way to stop the fury. When you feel an outburst coming, use what we call a *rage interrupter*. It can be a phrase or action. Some parents count to ten, and others take a deep breath. One dad bites his knuckle! Your authors' two favorites are (1) repeating "Love is patient, love is kind" (Becky) over and over; and (2) using a silent scream. (Lori turns away quickly and pretends to scream silently, and then turns back.) Rage interrupters replace the anger with a sense of control, calm, or humor. Find something that fits your personality, and use it to replace the anger.

Claim It

Next, verbalize the main emotion driving the anger. "I feel frustrated when you put your dirty shoes on the clean floor." Help your child do the same. Add to the mad, sad, glad vocab by saying, "I can see you're frustrated."

Speaking the main emotion is a valuable component in developing a plan for the upsetting issue. It is also a constructive way to communicate feelings. Anger is an indicator that something is amiss, and a plan needs to be put into place to deal with its cause. Dr. Scott Turansky, cofounder of the National Center for Biblical Parenting, explains, "Anger identifies problems but doesn't solve them."[6]

Resolve conflict and express anger in a healthy and constructive way. The words of Ephesians 4:26 lead to peace in the home: "'In your anger do not sin': Do not let the sun go down while you are still angry." This verse has helped my (Becky) family to resolve conflicts. Use these ideas to avoid sinful anger.

1. Identify your anger warning signs.

2. Use a rage interrupter.

3. Verbalize the emotion driving the anger.

4. Initiate a plan to deal with the issue.

5. If possible, keep a sense of humor!

"ANGER IDENTIFIES PROBLEMS BUT DOESN'T SOLVE THEM."[7]

THE SLOW BURN

Think of behavior that brings you to the point of anger. That is a hot spot. One of my (Becky) hot spots, one that would push me over the edge, was an issue with the stroller and one of its occupants. Minnesota winters bring lots of snow and ice. To avoid the slippery sidewalks, I would often go to the mall to walk. With a double stroller, both my baby and my toddler could ride. The problem was my two-year-old wanted to

122

walk, no, run. We would start off walking side by side, and then he would take off running in the opposite direction!

So, what's a mom to do? Chase down the escapee. My fear and frustration shifted to anger. When I caught him, he would laugh. And that made my blood boil. I realized I needed a plan. The solution was fairly simple. He could walk if he held my hand. If he let go, there were no second chances; he rode in the stroller with the seatbelt tightly fastened.

What are your hot spots, noise, chaos, disobedience, or temper tantrums? Decide now to keep cool when anger rises. What actions can you take to keep the situation fun, or at least manageable, rather than frustrating? Be proactive and determine a plan to deal with ongoing issues.

TURN IT DOWN!

Parents often complain about kids and noise levels. Little kids have big voices. One mom said the loudness of her home was causing her a great deal of stress. First, the mom and I (Lori) discussed things that contributed to the loud factor that were not child-related: Television volume, the phone ringing, CD players, and adult voice volumes. The mom decided to turn off the TV when it wasn't in use, turn down the phone's ringtone, and lower the volume or decrease use of the CD player. Once the background noise level was reduced, she was able to lower her own voice. She didn't need to shout to be heard.

Training the children to quiet down was the next phase of the plan. Rougher and more physical play needed to be moved outdoors or to the basement, out of mom's earshot. They practiced closing rather than slamming doors; walking, rather than running; and using softer voices indoors. "Slow feet, indoor voice" was the rule. Whenever the kids began to yell, the mom used a nonverbal sign to remind them to take it down a couple levels. She lowered her hand, palm down, from the side of her body—head to chest—to signal quiet. The plan worked. Her home is now more peaceful.

CONTROLLED CHAOS

"Daddy's home!" "Mommy's back!" Coming together after being apart is an event celebrated by young children. There is nothing better than returning home and receiving a little kid greeting. Jumping into Daddy's arms and hugging Mom as she crosses the threshold into the house is good stuff!

This was the best time of the day for my (Becky) family when the boys were little. They would patiently peer out the window for my husband's car to pull into the driveway. Then they would race for the door. This became our "First Hug and Kiss" game. I would get the first kiss, and the boys would each hug a leg. Inevitably Scott would end up with one boy in the crook of each arm, snuggling both to his chest.

What could be problematic about this? Competition. Siblings may jostle to be the first one to give the big hello. This has the potential to erupt into a fight, each one jockeying for position. Being proactive will prevent this enthusiastic welcoming from becoming a negative issue. If you experience this in your home, then try this: Plan the greeting order with the kids. First, the spouse, then a group hug, followed by a few minutes of individual time with each child. By bringing order to chaos and taking control of the situation peace is established.

Temper Tantrums

Most parents in our parenting classes identify tantrums as number one on their hot spot lists. Remember the story at the beginning of the chapter about the woman and her preschooler? The mom had the right idea but used the wrong words. She attempted to control the outburst by leaving the scene (good idea if you are able to do this). But when she yelled, "You're not dragging me into your hell!" that is just what happened.

When a child is in the middle of a tantrum, it is the parent's responsibility not to get hijacked into the emotional angst the child is experiencing. The mom's words degraded the child. We all know the embarrassment of having a little one display out-of-control kicking and screaming in public. Try to focus on your controlled response as opposed to what you think other people are thinking. Stay calm. If you are able to leave the scene, do so. (Leave, not escape. Take the child, too!) Think back on what precipitated the tantrum so it can be avoided the next time you're out and about in similar circumstances.

I (Lori) recall one evening grocery shopping with only one of my kids. I treasured times alone with each child. I guess she didn't feel the same that night. Instead, she chose to have a tantrum. I was more annoyed than embarrassed. The tantrum thrower this day was the youngest of four and I'd developed pretty thick skin by this time. It was not an option for me to leave the store; my time was tight. I knew my daughter's tantrums came and went quickly, so this was likely to be short-lived. I continued to push the shopping cart with her in it. One fellow shopper was visibly perturbed. She kept turning around, shooting nasty looks first at my child and then at me. I transferred all my frustration and annoyance with my child's behavior to her. Rather than taking my normal route around the store, I decided to keep following her. She and I both got to experience the piercing screams for one full aisle. (I know! Not the best solution.)

A few kind customers gave me the universal "I've been there" look. I really appreciated the sympathy they showed. I planned never again to judge a frazzled mom. A demonstration of grace is the way to go.

Tantrums come in many forms: the I'm-hungry-hot-thirsty-tired tantrum; the I'm-frustrated-stressed-out-or-overwhelmed tantrum; the I-want-my-way tantrum; the I'm-not-ready-yet transitional tantrum; the just-'cuz-I'm-two- (or three, five, nine, fifteen) tantrum. We can't extinguish all tantrums, but we can set the stage for fewer explosions.

Determine the reason for a typical outburst. Running errands when your child is hungry or has missed a nap increases the probability of a temper tantrum. If your child is on the brink of learning a new skill, then his frustration level may be high. Break down new tasks so success is experienced bit by bit. If the child is having a fit in an attempt to get his way, then don't give in. Allow him some choices in order to prevent most power tantrums.

Transitional tantrums were toughest at my (Becky) house. A five-minute warning that a venue change was coming was good prescription for this type of tantrum. That gentle reminder helped my boys shift gears more easily.

There are some tantrums that cannot be avoided. Whatever the reason for the display, approach the outburst with grace and understanding. If your young one notices his emotions are affecting yours, he will believe he's in charge. Stay focused and in control. Just because the child is exhibiting his worst, the parent does not need to follow. Once the tantrum is full-blown, discussing anything with the child is out of the question. Know your child. If he feels out of control and has a great need to feel safe, a bear hug with your arms wrapped around his arms and chest for security is good. If your child is one that has a great need for power rather than security, *do not* use this technique because you may get hurt!

Instead, take control of the situation as the Coach and tell him to take the tantrum to his room, as if the tantrum is a separate entity. Then say, "When you're ready to leave the tantrum, you can come be with me." The child that is in the power mode will get the message and feel like he has more control. Viewing the tantrum as something he can break away from increases his ability to settle down. When the tantrum is over, it's over! When the child has gained control, this is the desired behavior, so reward him by allowing him to join the family. This positive reinforcement will encourage the child to settle down more quickly and attempt to regain self-control when angry. Once he has self-control, recognize it. The final step is to forgive and move forward. Even a young child can be taught self-control, a fruit of the Spirit (Galatians 5:22-23). Point out this positive attribute to your child and celebrate his success, thereby restoring the relationship.

> ## VIEWING THE TANTRUM AS SOMETHING HE CAN BREAK AWAY FROM INCREASES HIS ABILITY TO SETTLE DOWN.

PEACEFUL COOPERATION

Don't you just love tranquility at home? When everybody cooperates and works together, the home is a peaceful place. Mom and Dad, encourage cooperation by being clear and concise with directions and expectations. Be direct like the Controller, empathize like the Chum, encourage like the Coach, and support like the Consultant.

"Pick up your crayons and put them in the box" (Controller).

"I know you don't like it when you're not ready to put your things away. May I help you?" (Chum/Consultant).

"It's great when you help pick up your art supplies. I can see you're becoming more responsible" (Coach).

By using all four approaches the child knows what needs to be done, and he feels understood, loved, and appreciated. A cooperative spirit is fostered. Our goal is to be like our Father: "gracious and compassionate, slow to anger and abounding in love" (Nehemiah 9:17c).

KEEPING THE PEACE

Cooperation, quality time, acceptance, and compromise can increase peaceful and harmonious family relationships. "Blessed are the peacemakers, for they will be called sons of God" (Matthew 5:9). Peacemakers are relationship builders. Agitators are relationship busters.

Women are typically more tuned into relational things and the children's personal preferences than are men. Men, give your wife permission to offer ideas to you for building relationships with your children. You'll find she is pretty good at it.

Here's an example. "Sweetheart," she might say, "you're going to the hardware store. Sammy loves tools. Could he accompany you?" Often Dad is focused on getting the job done and may not think of a chore or errand as an opportunity for father-child time.

Women, give your husband the freedom *not* to complete every task on the honey-do list so he is able to spend time with the children. When presenting ways for father and youngster to spend time together, suggest but don't demand or nag. Be positive and encouraging. Husbands and wives, cooperate with each other to strengthen family ties.

In-laws play a key role in helping to build and maintain extended family relationships. More often than not, it's the women who God uses to glue families together. When we marry, we gain an additional family. There are times compromise is needed to keep the peace.

My (Becky) mother-in-law has been a wonderful role model in demonstrating how to love and accept a new woman on the scene. She's given me her son and bent over backward to include me as part of the family. I hope I'll be a mother-in-law one day. My prayer is that I love as I have been loved. I have a choice: to become a monster-in-law or a mother-in-love.

Family members cannot be fixed or fired. Peace can be found in building relationships by spending time together, compromising when necessary, accepting, and cooperating with each other.

> **PEACEMAKERS ARE RELATIONSHIP BUILDERS.**
> **AGITATORS ARE RELATIONSHIP BUSTERS.**

Spare the Rod, Spoil the Child?

Blending together two family experiences in terms of discipline, especially in regard to spanking, can be challenging. People have strong opinions on corporal punishment. Most Christian parenting professionals recommend spanking. Most secular experts do not. Our recommendation is that its proper use depends on a few factors.

Spanking can be used effectively within certain parameters. If you have physical abuse in your family of origin, avoid spanking. Old tapes will begin to play and the spanking will escalate. If you use spanking as your default discipline or as a means to express your anger, stop. Spanking should only be used under certain, well-defined situations. It's up to the parents to decide when to spank. Some families spank younger children for disrespect, others spank for unsafe behavior such as running into the street.

Before the spanking give a quick explanation: For example, "You're receiving a spanking for your safety." Then deliver the spanking immediately and swiftly, followed by a hug and love. Finish the training by saying, "We hold hands when we cross the street."

If your little one looks at you with defiant eyes and says, "That didn't hurt," your spanking days are over. When a child challenges a parent on the effectiveness of a spanking, the frequency and intensity of the spanking tends to increase. Often the parent will react by hitting again, a little harder. This scene will only continue because the child's spirit is hardened; he'll never give the parent the satisfaction of admitting the swat hurt. Also, if your child is over five years of age, spanking has run its course.

Choosing whether or not to spank and when to spank is a family decision in which both parents should be in agreement. Consistency between mom and dad is needed for punishment to be effective. Other methods of discipline, training, and punishment are listed in the "A–Zs of Cooperative Interaction" found in the appendix.

> **IF YOUR LITTLE ONE LOOKS AT YOU WITH DEFIANT EYES AND SAYS, "THAT DIDN'T HURT," YOUR SPANKING DAYS ARE OVER.**

PEACE BE WITH YOU

Peaceful moments seem few and far between when immersed in parenting young children. Strive to find those moments. A quiet game of Old Maid in front of the fire, a mesmerizing storybook read in a hammock with bodies curled together, an afternoon nap in a fort made of blankets are all peaceful moments to treasure.

Modeling a calm environment is a parent's responsibility, maintaining a calm home is everyone's duty. Children learn what they live each day. Know your hot spots. Be quick to listen, slow to speak, and slow to become angry. You'll notice a difference!

LOVE NOTES ON PEACE

LORI WRITES: I'll never forget the time I spanked when I was angry. That was one of the worst parenting moments. I felt physically ill. I vowed never to do that again.

BECKY WRITES: When my boys were young and anger began to creep into my spirit, distraction and deep breathing helped me. Since they loved to snuggle and be read to, I'd distract them with a "book break." Breathing deeply together also worked with my youngsters. "Take a deep breath," is still a catch phrase in my family.

QUESTIONS

1. What are your hot spots? What rage interrupter would work for you?
2. How will you turn down the volume in your home?
3. How can you prevent some tantrums? How will you handle the next outburst?

PARENTING TIPS

1. Use a rage interrupter rather than exploding in anger.
2. Help your child identify and name the emotion that precipitated his anger.
3. Encourage cooperation by being clear and concise with directions and expectations.

PRAYER

Lord Jesus,

You are the Prince of Peace. Thank You for Your peaceful presence in my home. Please help me to be a peace-filled parent. Impress upon me a desire to extinguish my angry behavior. Illuminate my hot spots and assist me in responding calmly. Allow my chosen rage interrupter to calm me quickly. Let my actions be a good example for my children. Help them to name their feelings and control their emotions. Give me wisdom to see how to prevent tantrums. Give me self-control when they occur.

In Your holy name,

Amen

**DO NOT BE QUICKLY PROVOKED IN YOUR SPIRIT,
FOR ANGER RESIDES IN THE LAP OF FOOLS.**

Ecclesiastes 7:9

CHAPTER 8

CHOOSE FORGIVENESS

LOVE ... KEEPS NO RECORD OF WRONGS.

1 Corinthians 13:5d

NOW WE'RE COOKIN'

The end was in sight. I (Becky) was so excited to complete the project. For weeks I had worked on creating a cookbook in honor of my grandmother's birthday. Relatives and friends had sent me their recipes, letters with fond memories, and photographs. The deadline loomed. I felt pressured to finish the job. Scott offered to take the boys out of town for the weekend, so I jumped at the chance to work without distractions. Although compiling the submissions was enjoyable, it was tedious. The dining room table was strewn with papers. The computer and printer were set up on either end and plugged into a power strip under the table. I spent the weekend going from one end of the table to the other, checking formatting, editing, and printing.

By Sunday evening the cookbook was almost done with just a few pages to go when the boys walked through the door. After listening to their exciting tales of the weekend, I eagerly showed Scott the work I'd done. Suddenly, the computer screen went blank!

"Oh no!" I gasped. "All that work! What's happening?" In my haste to keep the pace, I hadn't saved the last section. It was *gone*.

A small blond head appeared over the side of the table.

"Look at the orange light, Mommy. I can turn it on and I can turn it off." My four-year-old son had discovered the power strip.

Really? I was beyond frustrated. My son saw my reaction. His eyes began to fill with tears. He knew he had done something wrong, but he just wasn't sure what it was. Scott nudged me, and I went over and gave my boy a big hug.

"It's okay." Thankfully it was okay. Only a few pages were lost. I was able to redo and finish the book once my little guys were tucked in for the night, knowing no one was going to flip the switch.

I want my boys to grow up in a home where the attitude of forgiveness permeates family relationships. I need to forgive all mistakes my boys make; the innocent accidents and the intentional incidents. I hope they will forgive me too when I mess up.

REMEMBER WHEN

Like Mary, Jesus' mom, we treasure our memories (see Luke 2:51). Recalling favorite moments brings joy when we retell them. Laughter and warm feelings accompany those thoughts. Some recollections aren't so fond. Other thoughts, dark thoughts, can also creep into our minds regarding our children's or our own past words, choices, or actions.

We hold onto regret and remorse. *But God* tells us we are forgiven and to repent. We revisit past hurts and perhaps seek revenge. But God calls us to forgive and reconcile. We recall our kids' mistakes rather than forgive as the Lord forgives. *But God* promises He forgives and forgets. We receive mercy and grace from our Father rather than getting what we deserve.

> **OUR HEARTS SHOULD MIRROR JESUS' FORGIVENESS.**

GRACE AND FORGIVENESS

One fall evening, I (Lori) was making dinner, talking on the phone, and watching my kids play together in the next room. My husband was on his way home from work. The house was presentable and a fire was crackling in the fireplace. I felt content. *Okay, this is how I dreamed it would be.* I looked up from stirring the pot and noticed my four kids had joined hands and were playing Ring Around the Rosie near the fireplace. *Oh no, danger!* I thought. Just as I abruptly concluded my call, my youngest child flew away from her siblings and smacked her head on the brick hearth. Heads bleed a lot! I grabbed a kitchen towel, pressed it against my toddler's head, and instructed the older three to jump into the van. We moved at lightning speed. My seven-year-old, the oldest, held the cloth to the two-year-old's head as I drove to the hospital.

My second oldest bellowed, "I'm going to kill myself!" He was more upset than his bleeding sister. "Mom, I let go of her hand." He confessed through sobs.

"I'll be okay," his injured sister repeated.

My son felt remorse and regret for his youngest sister's injury. Although it was unintentional and no one was blaming him, he knew he bore some responsibility in the accident.

My toddler was stitched up and good as new. "See, I'm all better," she said as she gave her big brother a hug. The grace and forgiveness she extended helped him to heal as well.

The only way to move past remorse and regret is by taking responsibility and repenting. A loving way to respond to another's confession and repentance is with the gift of grace paired with a forgiving heart.

THE BARRIER

Confession is a big part of the forgiveness process. Relationship restoration cannot happen without it. In Psalm 139:23-24, the psalmist asks God to reveal his offensive ways. "Search me, God, and know my heart; test me and know my anxious thoughts. See if there is any offensive way in me, and lead me in the way everlasting." That's a pretty bold prayer in my (Lori) opinion. God wants us to be bold.

To be delivered from guilt, confession is part of the package. Mary Heathman, founder and executive director of Where Grace Abounds in Denver, Colorado, counsels many people in the area of forgiveness. She shares her perspective.

> The practice of confession used to be troublesome to me. The whole idea of coming before an all-knowing God to report to him what he already knew didn't make sense. It seemed that confession was an exercise in humiliation. If God really loves us so much, why would he put us through such a thing?

> Then a simple illustration caught my attention. A conference speaker told the story of a man who came home from a business trip a day earlier than expected. As he stepped up to his front door, he saw through the window that his wife was in the arms of another man. Stunned, he left and returned again the next day at the expected time. The speaker asked, "Now, he knows she was unfaithful, and she knows that she was unfaithful. Why do they need to talk about it?"

> The answer was obvious, of course they must talk. Trust had been broken, the relationship was damaged and in need of restoration. There would be distance between them until they talked about it.

> Suddenly confession made sense to me. God, who created us for relationship with him and each other, wants us to come quickly to him to restore the distance created between us by our sin. The process of restoring that relationship begins with an honest acknowledgement of the sin and turning away from it. The act of confession is the first step in repentance.[8]

This is why it is so important to seek forgiveness for wrongdoing in a family. Our kids are okay with parental mistakes, but they do need to hear us say, "I'm sorry," or "I was wrong." If we are unable to articulate this, there will be a barrier in our relationships with our kids.

Whoops!

Emotional, relational, and spiritual healing begins with confession. Deliverance comes from the confession and repentance of sin. By modeling admission of mistakes children are trained in how to confess. At first it sounds scary; admitting sin takes guts. The brave act of admission of guilt has the supernatural power to bring about relational wholeness. Provide a nonthreatening atmosphere in your home so your children will feel safe confessing their mistakes. Teach your children to own their mistakes by owning yours.

Lori and I urge parents to avoid excusing a youngster for his behavior. Instead, we coach moms and dads to train even a young child to say, "I'm sorry. Please forgive me." Have him express sorrow when he's done something wrong. A parent can't make a child actually feel sorry, but empathy can be encouraged. Do this by being the Consultant. Use the common phrase, "How would you feel if you were in _____'s shoes? How would you like to be treated?" Eventually, through consistent training, remorse over wrongdoing or hurting someone's feelings will be internalized.

Going from responsibility to restitution is a natural step. Restitution is healing for everyone. Making a wrong right soothes both parties. It's easy to figure out consequences for material problems. Have you heard of the House Rules? "Break it–fix it, borrow it–ask, use it–put it back, lose it–replace it." Those are common sense consequences. With restitution it's important for the punishment to fit the crime so connections between the actions and outcomes are established.

A mom gave this account of forgiveness and restitution: "My two children were playing with a group of neighborhood kids. The ages ranged from nine to twelve. They were playing baseball in a church parking lot. One of the boys had a pretty powerful swing. The hard ball sailed into a stained-glass window, shattering it.

"I have to say I was pretty proud of the children. I'm sure there was a huge temptation to run, but as a group they went into the church. Standing together they confessed to the pastor what had occurred. Thankfully, the church, being in the business of grace, provided forgiveness. But the children also had to pay for the replacement window."

Forgiveness plus restitution is a great learning experience.

AVOID EXCUSING YOUR CHILD FOR HIS BEHAVIOR.

TURN, TURN, TURN

Repentance is a little harder than restitution. A repentant heart chooses to turn from the sin and not make the mistake again. Repentance is a turning from sin, an about-face. John the Baptist said, "Produce fruit in keeping with repentance" (Matthew 3:8).

Don't you find it encouraging that God's people weren't perfect? The Bible gives many accounts of people of faith sinning and repenting. Scripture gives an honest picture of humanity. What habit do you slip into when frustrated? When I'm (Becky) exasperated or annoyed with my children, irritation creeps into my voice and the volume increases. I get "Mommy's mad voice." Afterward, I vow to keep my emotions in check. Am I always able to do so? No. But every time I resort back to that old pattern, I apologize, ask forgiveness, and pray for God's strength to overcome.

Paul comments on human sinful tendency in Romans 7:19: "For I do not do the good I want to do; no, the evil I do not want to do—this I keep on doing." Failure is the best opportunity for people to learn and implement change. This is when we are most teachable.

To avoid reactionary anger in a volatile situation, use a rage interrupter and apply the replacement technique, praying for peace and self-control to replace rage. We can repent when we have a soft heart and God's help.

**WITH A SOFT HEART AND GOD'S HELP,
WE CAN TRULY REPENT.**

INSTANT REPLAY

Hanging onto past regrets provides an ample amount of debilitating guilt. Having a keen memory for past offenses feeds bitterness. This also keeps us stuck in reverse, replaying the events in our mind. Bitterness is fostered when history is relived over and over. This hardens the heart. This is why Paul writes that love "keeps no record of wrongs." Looking forward with eyes focused on Jesus rather than looking in the rearview mirror is the solution. We've all had hurts in relationships. They cut deep. Lori told me that she's guilty of remembering past offenses better than recalling the last movie she saw. "Each heart knows its own bitterness" (Proverbs 14:10a). We revisit our pain. By bringing up past offenses we sometimes falsely believe we're punishing the person who has hurt us. In reality we're only hurting ourselves.

When difficulties arise in life, betrayal being among the worst, Jesus understands. Reconciliation takes two, but forgiveness, only one. Asking, "Why has this happened?" is futile. Instead, ask, "How can I respond in a way that honors God in this circumstance?" This question will help keep your anger in check after your youngster has disappointed you. When you make a mistake and respond in rage, begin to ask yourself how you will handle a similar situation differently in the future. Rather than replaying the bad (I'm guilty of this), start a new tape. There will be another time to practice your new approach. Count on it!

Following an incident where your child has made a poor choice, ask, "What can I learn from this?" It's important silently to recall things that have historically tempted your kids. That demonstrates wisdom. In doing so you may be able to prevent or avoid situations that could lead to trouble.

Instead of silently recalling the past we often remind our child of his mistakes, thus cementing the memory in his brain. In effect we're reinforcing the bad behavior we'd hoped to extinguish. Remember his bent, his disposition. Train your child for the acceptable behavior. The Consultant asks, "How will you do this differently next time?" Using a domineering approach, the Controller says, "Go to your room and think about what you have done wrong," which is not nearly as helpful as the

138

Consultant's question and can be harmful. Replaying an action in the mind reinforces the negative behavior and shames the child.

This is a perfect time to build a bridge with your son or daughter. Rather than making the child feel even worse, use the Chum tactic and tell him about a time you handled something poorly. What's the point of stating the obvious by saying, "You shouldn't have _____"? At this stage of the game he already knows what he's done wrong. Demonstrate humility and love by showing empathy. Don't *replay* any unacceptable behavior, yours or your child's. Allow room for learning a better way and make space for forgiveness.

> **REPLAYING AN ACTION IN THE MIND REINFORCES THE NEGATIVE BEHAVIOR.**

IT'S NOT OKAY

In her article "Soul Snacks," Robin Chaddock offers her epiphany regarding forgiveness:

> I think one of the most profound thoughts I have encountered on forgiveness is that saying, "I forgive you" is not the same as saying, "It's OK." We have the capacity to forgive while still recognizing that what was done to us was not all right, in the case of physical or verbal violence, malicious gossip, or meanness of any kind. That was a very freeing thought to me when a pastor shared it. It sets a dynamic of dignity and boundary for the victim, and allows them to move out of a victim mindset.[9]

Forgiveness *can* occur without reconciliation. This happens when a situation is seemingly resolved but the relationship is dissolved.

One mom described a toxic relationship her daughter had with another little girl. Her child and another student became fast friends in their second-grade classroom. The two of them were inseparable for the first half of the school year. Sleepovers and playdates happened regularly. When apart they would Instant Message one another while on the Internet. Over time the friend became jealous, possessive, and competitive.

The mother said the child became angry over other friends, family, schoolwork, and material items related to her daughter. Her anger manifested itself as stone cold silence for days in a row.

"Thankfully," the mother said, "my child would tell me what was going on. I tried to help her but felt at a loss. I did confer with the teacher about the situation. She promised to keep a watchful eye."

Nevertheless, one evening her daughter ran into the kitchen visibly shaken. Her friend had just threatened her in cyberspace.

The woman's husband spoke to the father of the other girl. To his credit the other dad talked to his daughter. She confessed to her father but she never made it right with the other girl.

"We spoke to our child," the mother of the threatened girl said, "and told her to forgive the other girl and put this behind her."

"I don't want to forgive her, Mom," the little girl said. "She scares me. I can't be her friend anymore. Besides she never said she was sorry."

Even though asking forgiveness was the right thing, the mother explained to her daughter, that didn't mean the other child had to ask for forgiveness in order to be forgiven. The mother said, "Forgiving someone happens in your own heart. But just because you forgive the other girl doesn't mean the friendship should continue. In fact it's best to be nice to her but not act like close friends."

It only takes one person to forgive but two to reconcile. When there is an issue of abuse, lack of repentance, and no restitution, it is best to put up clear boundaries in that relationship. Even little-kid friendships can be abusive. When one individual attempts to control another's time and relationships, it is time to set some healthy relationship limits. Sadly, unhealthy relationships are not uncommon and can be quite frightening. Pay close attention to your child's friendships.

FRUIT OF FORGIVENESS

How often are we to forgive? Peter asked Jesus if he should forgive his brother up to seven times. Think about it. One time, let alone seven, can be challenging. Jesus was so serious about forgiveness he answered, "I tell you, not seven times, but seventy-seven times" (Matthew 18:22).

So how can we get to the place where our heart is soft enough to forgive? Stormie Omartian, in her book *The Power of a Praying Parent*, states, "The best way to become forgiving is to pray for the person you need to forgive."[10] God has a way of changing our hearts when we pray! Feelings will follow actions. In making a choice to forgive, we do our part and leave the rest to God.

Forgiveness, like peace, is a matter of self-control. *Mind over emotion.* Choosing to forgive or asking for forgiveness requires determination and humility. Unforgiveness engulfs us in a sea of bitterness. The person suffering is the one unable to forgive. Freedom is found in forgiveness.

Forgiveness seems easier to give than to receive. Or rather, it's simpler to forgive someone else's wrong than to admit our own. Mom, dad, and kids need to admit to wrongdoing in order to restore their relationship with God. Our pride gets in the way, holding us captive. Forgiving others and asking for forgiveness are both important.

Without question, forgiveness is a difficult process. But the alternative is worse. Consider this passage from Matthew 6:14-15: "For if you forgive men when they sin against you, your heavenly Father will also forgive you. But if you do not forgive men their sins, your Father will not forgive your sins." Yikes!

> ### FORGIVENESS SEEMS TO BE MUCH EASIER TO GIVE THAN TO RECEIVE.

LOVE NOTES ON FORGIVENESS

LORI WRITES: I've heard parents say, "My child doesn't deserve a hug when he's behaved badly. He needs to learn a lesson." Oh! It hurts my heart to hear that. I understand the overwhelming frustration, but the only lesson the child will learn in this case is that love is conditional. *Please* don't withhold affection from your little guy as a means of punishment. Instead, train him in the preferred way to act and follow up with a big hug.

BECKY WRITES: The hardest person for me to forgive is me. When I mess up, I beat myself up because I usually know better. Even when it's an honest mistake, I'm upset. Apologizing and making amends helps. I know in my heart God forgives me. I just need to become better at forgiving myself.

QUESTIONS:

1. Why is it a poor parenting strategy to concentrate only on misbehaviors?

2. Describe a situation where your child learned from his mistakes.

3. How does the response "I forgive you" differ from "It's okay"?

PARENTING TIPS

1. Teach your child to admit mistakes.

2. Don't replay the child's mistake.

3. Train your child to ask for forgiveness following an apology.

PRAYER

Forgiving Father,

Give me a humble heart so I can admit when I'm wrong and forgive when I'm wronged. Grant me wisdom to learn from my mistakes. Soften my heart and dull my memory so I don't become bitter over past offenses. Reveal whom I need to forgive. Put a spirit of forgiveness in my home. I want to forgive as I have been forgiven. Change my heart. Amen

AS FAR AS THE EAST IS FROM THE WEST, SO FAR HAS HE REMOVED OUR TRANSGRESSIONS FROM US.

Psalm 103:12

Section Five

Love Has a Heavenly Perspective

Chapter 9

Choose Goodness

Love does not delight in evil.

1 Corinthians 13:6a

Moral Compass

"Lord," one little boy prayed, "if you can't make me a better boy, don't worry about it. I'm having a real good time like I am." This simple illustration makes me (Lori) laugh because it really captures the human condition.

Growing from naughty to nice, or at least better, requires something all people have. See if you can guess what it is. Here's a clue. People have it but animals don't. Answer: a conscience. How we are raised—cultural customs, family values, and faith—determine to what extent the conscience is developed. We all share the Adam-and-Eve gene. "There is no one righteous, not even one" (Romans 3:10b). We are all born with a propensity to sin.

Do you agree with the statement "We are under the delusion that we aren't so bad"? Becky and I do. I tend to grade my sin, concluding most of it is justifiable and acceptable. Sometimes I even put a respectable spin on it.

The conscience on its own is susceptible to falling back on emotions to dictate right from wrong. It needs God's Spirit to be an effective moral compass. Without the Holy Spirit to guide the conscience, it will be compromised, corrupted, or weakened. "My conscience confirms it through the Holy Spirit" (Romans 9:1b).

DEVELOPING THE COMPASS

When we examine developmental phases, we have a better understanding of how little kids view right and wrong. In the early stages of conscience development, babies determine good and bad according to how things feel. If it hurts, it's bad, or feels pleasurable, it's good. Hunger brings an ache. That's bad. Cry. Being fed and cuddled feels nice. That's good. Coo. (Personally I prefer things that feel physically good over things that feel bad, too. Don't you?)

Responding to your infant's needs communicates love and builds trust. A warm bottle, a dry diaper, and a sweet lullaby feel good. The parents act on the child's need, and the little one reacts to Mom or Dad's attention, and then Mom or Dad responds back. This sets the stage for growth of trust, an important component in developing a conscience. The child begins to understand his behavior affects his parents.

Unfortunately, the feel-good element of the early phase isn't the best indicator of right and wrong. Too bad it's not that simple. In Hebrews 11:25, the author points out that Moses "chose to be mistreated along with the people of God rather than to enjoy the fleeting pleasures of sin." We're not all like Moses. Wrong can feel so right. Things that are right may bring more pain than pleasure. Waiting to be served rather than grabbing another's snack may not feel good, but it is right to wait. Not taking other people's things is a value that needs to be learned. Obedience training is the second stage of conscience development. We need to teach our kids acceptable and unacceptable behaviors.

> OBEDIENCE TRAINING IS THE SECOND STAGE OF CONSCIENCE DEVELOPMENT.

No Wrong, Know Wrong

Our little guys don't need to be taught wrong. Wrong they get. As cute and sweet as our children are, the ability to do wrong comes naturally. Charles Swindoll says, "Every child has the potential of becoming a study in hostility…a heartache…a model of wickedness. There's no denying it—parents must deal with the evil that rests in their children's lives. Those who fail to do so consistently and wisely will face a future of misery."[11]

On that note, let's talk about cultivating goodness. Regularly encouraging desirable behavior in your kids is one of the greatest things a parent can do. God created our little ones to want to please Mommy and Daddy. The young child that prefers negative attention over positive is the exception. By stating the expected behavior, reinforcing the desired behavior, and correcting the unacceptable actions, you are providing obedience training. This is where consistency counts.

When giving correction, don't give the message that the child is bad, weak, or stupid. Be positive and train him with love and grace. For example, "Don't grab that cookie from me. Are you an animal?" is a correction combined with shame rather than love and grace.

Rather, say something like this: "*Oops!* Let's try again. I'll hand you the cookie and you can gently take it from my hands. After you take it say, 'Thanks, Mommy.'" (The Coach says, "Try again"; the Controller tells specifically how; and the Chum spurs on the necessary tenderness in the correction.)

Toddlers and preschoolers need very specific instructions. Don't let them guess how to act. They will most likely guess incorrectly. Tell two- to three-year-olds *exactly* what to do. When sitting down for dinner, say, "Sit in your chair. Use a quiet voice. I'll help you with your food."

Four-year-olds respond well to physical and social limitations but need reminding. "Our rule is to ask before using someone else's things." Talk about and reinforce appropriate behavior and family rules.

We don't want to raise kids that make excuses, blaming others for their problems or minimizing wrongs. Correcting with love will help them avoid this reaction.

146

INSTRUCTIONS NOT INCLUDED

It's hard to do right if we don't know what constitutes wrong. (I guess that's why God gave us the Ten Commandments.) Can you imagine if you had never seen an outdoor playset or even a picture of one, yet you had to put one together? But then imagine if the box that held the parts said, "Instructions *not* included." It would be an impossible task.

Our kids have no idea how to behave because they haven't had experience or exposure to many situations. They won't intuitively know good or bad words and actions. Unless they are guided, they will not be able to behave well.

Put your behavioral expectations in writing. Write down your family's list of acceptable behaviors and post them on the refrigerator or some other easily visible spot. Keep the list to five rules or less. Writing and posting the rules adds importance. (Even if your kids are too young to read, do this. I like Becky's idea of using pictures to show appropriate behaviors.) Here's the most important part of this exercise: State your ideas in the *positive*. Write, for example, "Use an inside voice," instead of saying, "Don't yell in the house."

Becky's family worked on the rules list when her younger boy was a toddler and her eldest a preschooler. I did a double take when I saw number five: "We 'poo' in the potty." Good rule!

DO-GOODERS

In addition to putting appropriate behavior in writing, simply state expectations: "When we go to Grandma's, you can look at all her pretty things while you keep your hands by your side (or in your pockets)." Notice how this expectation was also stated in the positive. If you were to say, "Don't touch Grandma's breakable stuff," then that would be the very first thing the child would do. Stop a problem before it starts by being proactive. Don't assume your child won't touch all the beautiful sparkling treasures Grandma has on display. Anticipate, then prevent.

Parents will express exasperation when visiting another family's home if the child begins to jump on the furniture. When asked, "Is your son or daughter allowed to do this at home?" more often than not the answer is a sheepish "Yes." The logical solution is to stop allowing this. By clearly voicing what you expect ("We *sit* on the furniture") and reinforcing those expectations ("Sit or get down"), much of the mystery regarding acceptable and unacceptable behavior disappears.

PLAY BY THE RULES

When your child begins to understand behavior limits and starts to apply them, learning to play games by their rules will be more successful. Playing games according to the rules is a fun way to reinforce the concept of limits. But attempting to play a game by the rules with a toddler is an exercise in futility.

"Two-year-old rules." My (Lori) three older kids got in the habit of defining how a game was to be played if the youngest wanted to join in. They became frustrated trying to teach her the rules for Candy Land. She was too young to play properly. Sometimes I'd help out while she sat on my lap. As partners we would move the game piece together. If I wasn't a part of the mix and it was at the beginning of the game, her siblings would adjust, two-year-old style, by allowing her to move her piece wherever she wanted. Soon she'd become distracted with something else and their game could begin in earnest.

WHY, WHY, WHY?

Yep, it's tiresome to hear the word *why* over and over. Rather than sighing in frustration, try to look at the question this way. The word *why* in the context of behavior is the clue that the child's conscience is developing.

Around three and a half to four years old abstract thinking regarding right and wrong, discernment, begins to develop. Parents will hear the question "Why?" *a lot*. This is the perfect time to earnestly begin emphasizing family values, morals, and faith.

Let's add onto the cookie scene presented earlier in the chapter.

"*Oops!* Let's try again. I'll hand you the cookie and you can gently take it from my hands. After you take it say, 'Thanks, Mommy.'"

"Why?"

"It's respectful to be gentle and grateful."

"Why?"

"Respect is love."

"Why?"

"God teaches us that."

"Why?" (Here is where the *why* can get annoying)

This could go on and on. Once you have concluded your training, wrap it up.

"Let's try it with respect. Be gentle. Say thank you."

In this exchange the values of respect, gentleness, love, gratefulness, and God-honoring behavior have all been discussed and enforced. You have just poured lots of goodness into your child's growing conscience.

> ### THE WORD WHY IS THE CLUE THAT
> ### THE CHILD'S CONSCIENCE IS DEVELOPING.

PICK YOUR POISON

Here's something that may be a bit unsettling: Our conscience alone isn't enough to fight sin, and our feelings can mislead us. We need God's Word and the Holy Spirit to guide our thinking and train our conscience. Jerry Bridges, author of *Respectable Sins*, explains why the power of the Spirit is necessary: "Practically speaking, we live under the controlling influence of the Spirit as we continually expose our minds to seek and obey the Spirit's moral will for us as revealed in Scripture."[12]

God's Spirit and His Word are the tools we have been given to resist our sinful nature. We each have the propensity to sin and our own special weaknesses to temptation. As it says in James 1:14-15, "But each one is tempted when, by his own evil desire, he is dragged away and enticed. Then, after desire has conceived, it gives birth to sin; and sin, when it is full-grown, gives birth to death." The temptation itself isn't sinful; it's the action that follows. Our emotions can rule our body and mind rather than our conscience that is led by the Holy Spirit and Scripture.

Begin to arm your young ones by reading about biblical characters. Two heroes in the book of Genesis are Noah and Joseph. Both stayed strong during great adversity. Becky and I also love the accounts of David, Elijah, and Daniel in the Old Testament. They make for exciting reading: standing up to a giant, confronting powerful leaders, obeying God even in the presence of harsh persecution. Cool stories! Heroes all flawed yet all men of God.

> OUR CONSCIENCE ALONE ISN'T ENOUGH
> TO FIGHT SIN, AND OUR FEELINGS CAN MISLEAD US.

STOP

Get into the habit of noticing when your child is hungry, angry, lonely, or tired. These are weak moments, times when he is most likely to behave badly. When he teaches on temptation, Charles Stanley uses the acronym H.A.L.T. (which stands for *hungry, angry, lonely, or tired*) to help determine weak moments. If your child has something that tends to trigger poor behavior, change the venue to avoid the trigger or recognize the trigger and be aware.

Observing and helping our little ones avoid trouble spots is necessary as they begin to build the trait of goodness in their developing conscience. "Watch and pray so that you will not fall into temptation" (Matthew 26:41a). Pray that your children choose goodness.

Character Training

Think of character traits you would like to instill in your child. Patience, kindness, generosity, joy, compassion, gratefulness, perseverance, discernment, humility, self-control, and grace are all highly desirable qualities. Pray for opportunities to develop these characteristics in your child. And pray for teachable moments. If you notice your child has a bent toward jealousy, you could pray in this way: "Lord, please replace my child's jealousy with contentment." Becky and I call this the "replacement technique." Note the character deficiency and pray for a godly trait to replace it.

Combining prayer with training is the most effective way to encourage goodness in your child. For example, if you'd like to increase your child's ability to be gentle to animals, then take the time to show him how to properly approach and pet a dog or cat. Your own pet is best. If the animal belongs to another, then ask permission. Talk about how the animal loves to be stroked with the palm of the hand. Show how to apply minimal pressure and avoid the face and paws. Practicing this type of interaction is beneficial to both child and critter! Then pray that gentleness replaces roughness.

> **Note the character deficiency and pray for a godly trait to replace it.**

Tattletale

Some kids take on the job of policing siblings or peers while beginning to grasp the concepts of good and bad, right and wrong. As kids are prone to do, they can go to the extreme, reporting the tiniest of infractions. When I taught first grade, this was an ongoing challenge. I found the best way to curb some of this behavior was to ask a question before the tattling started.

"Mrs. Wildenberg! Emily…"

"Stop a minute, Luke. Will what you say get someone into trouble or out of trouble?"

Teachers and parents alike need to be informed quickly if there is a safety issue. This was the distinction I used with my five- and six-year-old students. *Telling* is a report that gets someone out of a harmful or hurtful situation. *Tattling* is a means to hurt the person being reported. Telling or tattling, that's the question. Kids can learn to discern the difference.

BAD TO THE BONE

Children also tend to go to the extreme when observing behavior, generalizing that the person doing the behavior is a bad person. When youngsters have been taught smoking is bad, they may believe the smoker is an evil person. (By using the word *unhealthy* rather than *bad* this problem is alleviated.)

In a child's frame of reference the designation of *bad* can also include activities to which he hasn't been exposed or in which he has not been allowed to participate.

My (Becky) six-year-old son had a friend over to play. Since it was raining outside, the buddies headed for the family room. The friend stopped short, staring at my husband's white-tailed deer mount on the wall. "What's that?" he asked.

"My dad's buck," my son proudly told his pal.

"Where did he get it?" he asked, each word carefully chosen.

"He shot it."

"Your dad shoots animals?" the boy said. "Only bad people have guns and shoot animals." He was clearly agitated.

My boy whirled around. "My dad is not bad! He's a good hunter!" It was time for me to step in and redirect. "How about setting up the train set, boys?"

They abandoned the conversation and enjoyed the rest of the afternoon playing with the trains.

When the boy's mom picked up her son, she and I discussed the interaction. Her family didn't hunt. They didn't bear any malice or have any negative feelings about those who did. Her son had made the jump

152

from hunting to "bad people with guns" all on his own. Left to their own means, children will draw their own conclusions. Guidance is needed.

Forbidden Words

Potty talk, nasty words, and swearing can create a lot of commotion when spoken by a little person. Verbalizing words that describe bodily functions seems to be the most fun. This type of language typically begins around toilet-training times and continues into age four. (Sometimes this can go even longer.)

The use of obscenities, swearing, and cussing may occur around the age of eight. In any of the instances not making a huge deal out of the utterances is the wisest approach. Simply say, "We use other words in our home."

In the preschooler, if this type of talking persists, first try ignoring the utterances, since the child's motivation is typically a need for attention. The less attention, the sooner the behavior will be extinguished. If the offensive words have become habitual, then take the child aside and help him come up with some other words to use. Reinforce the new vocabulary. Train, retrain, correct, and punish if necessary.

If your elementary child has picked up some swear words, discuss why that language is offensive. Talk about polite, acceptable, and more effective means to communicate. Bring in the idea of how we show respect for God and others by our word choices. "Nor should there be obscenity, foolish talk or coarse joking, which are out of place, but rather thanksgiving" (Ephesians 5:4).

Kids will copy both friends and parents when it comes to word choices. I (Becky) had a student in my kindergarten class who consistently used a foul word after making a mistake. After many interventions, I finally called the parent.

"Well," the parent said, "I don't know where the **** he's heard that before! I'll talk to him. Thanks for calling."

It has been said that children are our best chaperones. Our words and actions are always making an impact on our kids. Positive and negative. "You teach what you know but you reproduce what you are," John Maxwell has said.[13]

At Least I Don't Do That

We love to put a nice spin on our sin, justifying our actions by grading sin. We can be easily fooled into thinking that it's honorable to choose the lesser of two evils. "Well, I'm not gossiping, I'm just listening," we might say. Or "I won't lie, but I'll just leave out a few details." The word *just* seems to be one of the most innocuous words in the English language. It sneaks into our conscience and leads us to believe that if we *just* take part a tiny bit, we aren't really involved in the sinful behavior. That's all the enemy needs, a tiny entry point. Charles H. Spurgeon spoke these wise words, "Of two evils, choose neither."[14]

There are four categories of ways to live and make decisions. They each involve actions and attitudes.

1. The right way with the right heart: Jesus willingly dies on the cross for us.

2. The right heart but the wrong way: Moses kills the guard who had beaten the slave.

3. The right way but with the wrong heart: Jonah reluctantly goes to Nineveh to warn the people about their sin.

4. The wrong way and the wrong heart: Abraham lies about Sarah being his wife because of his own fear.

Guide your six- to nine-year-old kids in honestly evaluating their own motivations and behaviors. Teach them to talk to God before they act. Have them ask themselves, "Does this action help or hurt someone? Is this true? Is it kind?" These are good questions to ask before acting or speaking.

Nurture versus Nature

"The spirit is willing, but the flesh is weak" (Mark 14:38b). Goodness is nurtured through obedience, a developed sense of right and wrong, and through the Holy Spirit. Prayer is a large component to fostering good over evil. All of us struggle with sin nature. Due to the sin nature parents can't be lax about the important task of partnering with the Lord in encouraging their child's character development. The Holy Spirit is the ultimate and ongoing conscience developer. Pray that the Spirit speaks loud and clear to your young one and that your child attends to that still small voice. Prayer, talking, training, and modeling are ways parents can encourage a healthy conscience in kids.

Love Notes on Goodness

Lori writes: One afternoon while driving, I was talking with God about a situation in which I behaved badly. Directly in front of me was a car with a bumper sticker that read, "Before you act, talk to me.—God." As I was writing this chapter the Lord reminded me how often I do it wrong and how He responds to me with grace, love, and sometimes humor.

Becky writes: My kids know *correction is not rejection*. When my boys act inappropriately, it's my job to retrain with love. My mission is to change the behavior, not squash my child's self-esteem. My family is very gregarious and affectionate, so corrections generally come with a big hug and a few kisses.

Questions

1. How will you respond to your child's repeated, "Why?"

2. How will you squelch foul language in your child (and in yourself)?

3. What are your triggers before falling prey to temptation? What are your child's triggers?

Parenting Tips

1. State behavioral expectations clearly.

2. Use the replacement technique when praying with and for your children.

3. Pray for the Holy Spirit to lead your child's conscience.

PRAYER

Father in heaven,

You are goodness, pure goodness. Thank You for the Holy Spirit's power to assist me in raising my children and teaching them right from wrong. Give each of us strength in tempting situations. While You are developing my children's character, develop mine. Draw me to Your Word so I know what is pleasing to You. Help me to lead well.

In Your name I pray,

Amen

GOD, HAVE MERCY ON ME, A SINNER.

Luke 18:13c

Chapter 10

Choose Truth

Love rejoices with the truth.

1 Corinthians 13:6b

Sowers of Seeds

My first-grade son came home from school one day with downcast eyes. He was usually a perky kid with a constant bounce in his step.

"What's up?" I asked him as he plopped his backpack on the bench.

"At recess today, we were talking about church. Sam told me he doesn't believe in Jesus."

"What do you think of that?"

"Mom, I feel sorry for him. I told him all about Jesus and he still doesn't believe."

I hugged my courageous son, pulled him down on the bench next to me, and told him the parable of the sower (see Matthew 13:1-23). "You planted a seed today," I said. "Maybe you'll see it grow into faith, maybe not. Just know you planted a seed for Jesus today."

Christians, especially Christian parents, are in the seed-planting business. Seeds of faith need to be sown daily into the lives of our children, teaching Jesus as the Way, the Truth, and the Life (John 14:6). Biblical truth is the solid foundation they will need to depend on throughout life.

Lori and I are passionate about faith development, imparting truth to our children. Parents are the spiritual leaders of the home, guiding and leading their children to Jesus. This is done through intentional teaching times as well as spontaneous learning. Modeling a Christ-like life is a priority. Children may not always do what you say, but they will *always* do what you do! In her book about children and prayer, Betty Shannon Cloyd says, "If we learn to practice the presence of God in all that we do and live as to reflect the spirit of God, these unspoken actions speak volumes to children."[15]

BIBLICAL TRUTH IS THE SOLID FOUNDATION UPON WHICH WE STAND WITH OUR FAMILIES.

LABOR OF LOVE

The faith of a young child begins experientially through the rituals and religious traditions as observed and acknowledged by his family. As he experiences Easter, baptism, communion, and other traditions within the family's faith, he will learn their importance through participation. If Christmas is merely a holiday for Santa Claus and toys instead of a celebration of the birth of his Savior, Christian faith will not grow in a child. In Ephesians 6:4b parents are called to raise children in the "training and instruction of the Lord." The responsibility of nurturing faith lies with the parent not just during holidays but every day.

Many moms and dads in our parenting classes admit they don't feel comfortable teaching their children about God and the Bible. "Where do I start?" they ask. "What if I don't know the answer to my child's question?"

Lori and I encourage them, and you, to learn with your child. "I don't know," you might say, "but let's find out together." This is an honest answer. Trust in the power of the Holy Spirit to guide you as you lead your children. The Lord gave you a divine appointment in raising your children. He will thoroughly equip you. Be assured and encouraged!

P.O.W.W. SUPPORT NETWORK

God's equipping is necessary because parents alone cannot successfully build faith values into their children. I use the acronym P.O.W.W. to help parents remember the components of a complete support network: *prayer, other Christians, worship,* and the *Word.*

Let's begin with the **P**, which stands for prayer, communicating through speaking and listening to God. Think back to the early days when you and your spouse were first getting to know one another. Time to talk was necessary to get acquainted. The same goes for building a relationship with the Lord. Encourage your child to get to know God intimately through prayer.

Rote prayers are a simple way for young children to pray. By age four, a child can begin to use his own words to speak with God. Teaching a child to pray is valuable. You may not always be able to be there for your child, but God is. Use these prayer models to get started at any age.

1. ACTS Format: Adoration, confession, thanksgiving, and supplication is an easy-to-remember phrase that reminds us of the essential elements of every prayer. Begin prayers by praising God (adoration), so the child will focus on the Lord. Continue with his need to confess and be thankful before he ends with asking God for his wants (supplication).

2. Alphabet Prayer: Pray, listing the attributes of God in alphabetical order: *A*-almighty, *B*-beautiful, *C*-caring, *D*-divine, *E*-eternal, and so on.

3. Smile Prayer: Use your child's face to pray for godly characteristics: mouth to speak kind words, eyes to see others in need, and ears to hear the voice of God.

4. Scripture: Read and pray Bible passages that coincide with a particular need. A concordance is a handy tool for this type of prayer. For example, with a thankful heart, a child can pray the words of Psalm 9:1: "I will praise you, O LORD, with all my heart; I will tell of all your wonders."

5. The Lord's Prayer found in Matthew 6:9-13: Even young children can memorize the prayer Jesus taught the disciples.

Get ideas from other parents and children. One dad said his boys, while at a friend's home for dinner, heard the friend end his dinner prayer by thanking God for the hands that prepared the meal. Now they do likewise. It's a thoughtful addition to table grace.

Next is **O**. Other Christians serve as role models and teachers. Think of the people you spend the most time with as a family. Youngsters are influenced by not only their own peers but also the parent's friends. Strong Christians in a child's life will make a godly impression.

W is for worship. Corporate worship with a body of believers at a local church provides an expression of faith and the opportunity to belong to something bigger than oneself. Expert instructors, pastors, and lay teachers teach the Word of God. According to a friend, there are two extremes in parents. The "DIY parents" (do it yourself) single-handedly teach their kids everything they need to know about the Bible. Then there are the "Dry Cleaning parents" who drop their soiled children on the doorstep of the church and expect the Sunday school teachers to clean them up in an hour. Shoot for the center of the two extremes. Your church is your resource.

The final **W** is the Word of God. The Bible is our daily bread and the communication tool God most often uses to guide His children. Give children Bibles that are developmentally appropriate and interesting. Children's Bibles are wonderful and include pictures to enhance the stories. The Bible is a life-giving tool on which we can depend. "For the LORD gives wisdom; from his mouth come knowledge and understanding" (Proverbs 2:6). Wisdom, knowledge, and understanding are all found in the Word.

P.O.W.W. is a set of power tools. Teaching your children about the Lord shouldn't feel so overwhelming when you remember P.O.W.W. Keep that tool chest close at hand!

Heaven-sent Bible-teaching Tips

Get set up to be encouraged and equipped as you walk with your child on his journey of faith by using the following section's tips for Bible teaching. In living to honor God, we can train children about the Bible by using the acronym B.I.B.L.E., which stands for *basic instructions before leaving earth*. Knowing God's precepts, His absolute truth, provides soul revival and joy.

> The law of the LORD is perfect, refreshing the soul. The statutes of the LORD are trustworthy, making wise the simple. The precepts of the LORD are right, giving joy to the heart. The commands of the LORD are radiant, giving light to the eyes. The fear of the LORD is pure, enduring forever. The decrees of the LORD are firm, and all of them are righteous. They are more precious than gold, than much pure gold; they are sweeter than honey, than honey from the honeycomb (Psalm 19:7-10).

When teaching biblical truths to your children, keep these pointers in mind:

1. Find a time that works for your family. Bedtime is often good for little ones. A breakfast lesson provides a great start to the day for the elementary school age child.

2. Begin with stories. Jesus taught in parables and stories, so follow His example.

3. Short people = short lessons: The younger the child, the shorter the Bible passage that should be used.

4. Slide between Coach and Consultant mode by asking questions. "What did you like about the story?" Move to application questions with children over five years of age. For example,

"The little boy helped Jesus by sharing his lunch of bread and fish. What are some ways you can be helpful to others?"

5. Repeat the lessons. Children will not understand it all the first time. Think of how Bible passages take on deeper meaning as you grow closer to Jesus. Children are the same. In different life situations the Bible will comfort and guide.

God's Word became sweeter than honey when my (Becky) dad, affectionately called Doc, was sick with cancer. When God took him home, my boys had many questions about heaven. A friend suggested Randy Alcorn's book *Heaven for Kids*. The book addresses the many facets of heaven from a biblical perspective and uses *The Chronicles of Narnia* by C. S. Lewis for the comparison. Will we laugh? Will there be animals in heaven? Will we have real bodies in heaven? Yes, yes, and yes! All these questions and more are addressed from Scripture.[16] We have promises from God of life eternal, straight from the Word of God. Relying on God's Word will light the way, always.

DAILY DOSES

Today's parents desire to provide as many experiences and opportunities as possible for their kids. How many parents include God or the Bible in everyday life and not just on Sundays? Scott and I struggled with this when our boys were young. Sunday school was a treat for them, even as little boys. But the nagging question was, how do we weave our faith into daily life?

We coined the term *eternal moments* to describe the concept of how we incorporate faith lessons into everyday activities. When at the zoo, Scott would point out the great variety of animals God made. When at the grocery store, I would ask the boys to identify the beautiful colors of the fruits and vegetables God created. Magnificent sunsets, multicolored leaves, and raindrops all became eternal moments for sharing the grandeur of God. Reading Scripture enhanced these moments. For example, after witnessing a rainbow following a storm, we read about the promise of the first rainbow God created (Genesis 9:12-17). Eternal moments make an ordinary day special by including God. In *Empowered Parents*, Becky and I wrote, "They are the moments that we instill our own love of the Lord in our children. Eternal moments are the times we spend enriching our souls and minds or teaching spirituality to our children.[17]

ETERNAL MOMENTS PROVIDE A DAILY DOSE OF GOD.

STEEPED IN TRUTH

We want our children to be steeped in or surrounded by the Word. Why? There is only one way to heaven. This claim is not politically correct, but Jesus wasn't politically correct in His time either. Salvation is in Christ alone. "Salvation is found in no one else, for there is no other name under heaven given to mankind by which we must be saved" (Acts 4:12).

Deuteronomy 6:5-9 is just for parents. "Love the LORD your God with all your heart and with all your soul and with all your strength. These commandments that I give you today are to be on your hearts. Impress them on your children. Talk about them when you sit at home and when you walk along the road, when you lie down and when you get up. Tie them as symbols on your hands and bind them on your foreheads. Write them on the doorframes of your houses and on your gates." At both the Wildenberg and Danielson homes, we have Scripture verses as art on the walls. Look in each room of your home. Is there evidence of your family's faith? Be creative. Let your house be a home where Jesus, the Absolute Truth, is proclaimed as Lord and Savior.

SO SAD

There are people in the world who claim there is no absolute truth. Ironic. The statement itself is a declaration of an absolute truth. Even as early as elementary school, our children may be challenged in their faith. During a family dinner, one fourth-grader shared about her day. Her teacher had discussed Buddhism, which was not part of the curriculum. The dinnertime conversation gave the parents a glimpse into their youngster's day and a window into the teacher's possible belief system.

This presented an opportunity for the parents to discuss Buddhism and how it differs from Christianity. Rather than being fearful, the parents armed their child with knowledge and truth. Rather than being angry, the parents were now aware of the instructor's slant on life and were able to communicate this to their child.

Be the Chum, Coach, and Consultant listening to and talking with your children. If the conversation regarding Buddha hadn't happened, the child would have been left to her own devices to process the classroom discussion.

Kids ask tough questions about the origin of life and God. Neil Olsen, family friend and expert in fossils and dinosaurs, took time to sit down with my (Becky) sons and discuss paleontology from a biblical perspective. He explained how dinosaurs were created by God and are recorded in the Bible as well as fossilized rock. The boys were taken with the conversation God had with Job about dinosaurs: "Look at Behemoth, which I made along with you and which feeds on grass like an ox" (Job 40:15). Science and archeology will always prove God's existence because they are "HisStory." (Read Job 40-41.)

Parents can provide further aid by being in the know regarding school curriculum. Attend curriculum night at your child's elementary school. Know what is being taught, so you can enhance the study at home or correct the teaching if necessary.

Blind Trust

We often take the teaching in religious institutions and organizations for granted. If a cross is displayed, we assume the teaching is true. As 2 Peter 2:1b-c says, "There will be false teachers among you. They will secretly introduce destructive heresies, even denying the sovereign Lord." False teaching and false teachers exist in the church.

Before joining a church or having your kids attend a faith-based event, know the organization's foundational beliefs. As a family, we've (Lori) had two experiences in mainline churches where Christ's miracles were passed off as coincidence and manipulation. The first was in a sermon from Matthew 8:28-34. The passage describes the healing of two demon-possessed men by Jesus, telling how Jesus cast out the demons into a large herd of pigs. The pastor, as an aside to these verses, said, "We now know the men had epilepsy. And when Jesus arrived on the scene their seizures stopped."

Years later, in an entirely different church and state, a guest speaker in the pulpit told the congregation he'd just returned from a large conference. In his sermon he said how he'd been confused and the math didn't add up when he'd studied the miracle of feeding the five thousand in John 6. The minister explained that due to the conference he was now enlightened as to how this occurred. He continued, "It wasn't Jesus multiplying the food; it was the people sharing. They were pulling hidden food out of their cloaks." The speaker reduced the miracle to an old children's story, *Stone Soup*.

Both of these preachers denied Christ's miracles with a human explanation. Jesus claimed to be God. "Believe me when I say that I am in the Father and the Father is in me; or at least believe on the evidence of the miracles themselves" (John 14:11). He performed miracles to encourage belief. Jesus either is who he said he was, or he's a liar or crazy. He never claimed to be a good man. Good men don't lie to manipulate people. Pay attention. Watch for leaders who may subscribe to false doctrine and lead your children astray. False teaching permeates mainstream Christianity as well as other places. Investigate before you or your child join a new church or participate in a religious activity. Make certain the organization speaks truth.

> INVESTIGATE BEFORE YOU OR YOUR CHILD JOINS A NEW CHURCH OR PARTICIPATES IN A RELIGIOUS ACTIVITY. MAKE SURE TRUTH IS TAUGHT.

LEGACY OF FAITH AND LOVE

What will be your legacy? Take another peek at the Family of Origin Assessment in the introduction. What faith practices will you keep from your past, what will be added, and what will be discarded? Use the techniques listed in this book to craft your legacy, one of faithfulness.

Listed below are some ideas for you to begin the process.

1. Teach children to believe *in* God and to *believe* God because He is trustworthy. Model trustworthiness and faithfulness.

2. In a crisis turn to God. "Such is the destiny of all who forget God; so perishes the hope of the godless. What they trust in is fragile; what they rely on is a spider's web. They lean on the web, but it gives way; they cling to it, but it does not hold" (Job 8:13-15). Talk about your dependence on the Lord in times of trouble.

3. Love unconditionally, just like the Father. "Let your face shine on your servant; save me in your unfailing love" (Psalm 31:16).

4. Pray without ceasing. "Be joyful always, pray continually, give thanks in all circumstances; for this is God's will for you in Christ Jesus" (1 Thessalonians 5:16-18).

5. Become Christ-like. C. S. Lewis stated this point eloquently: "The more we get what we now call 'ourselves' out of the way and let Him take us over, the more truly ourselves we become."[18]

Always the Truth

Have you noticed truth today is fabricated, twisted, or entirely absent? Our own experiences and perspectives cloud the truth. But there is hope in the shifting sand. As believers in Jesus Christ, we have the gift of the Holy Spirit to aid us in discerning the truth. Jesus tells us he is Truth, absolute truth. Biblical truth is the solid foundation upon which we can stand with our families. Spend time assisting your child on his journey to the cross. Incorporate eternal moments. Seep the Word of God into him. Leave a legacy of faith. This is the single most important investment you will ever make.

Many years ago John Crosby, my (Becky) senior pastor, said, "My greatest joy will be welcoming my daughters at the gates of heaven." What a beautiful day of celebration and a legacy of their faith.

Love Notes on Truth

Lori writes: When my son was in second grade, he couldn't decide between being a pro football player or a pastor when he grew up. He knew he'd have to choose one or the other because both worked on Sunday. This is one of my favorite memories.

Becky writes: I love my church. Walking through the door feels like entering my own home. Through this body of faith, my family's P.O.W.W. network has been strengthened. When there have been bumps in the road, the four support systems that help my family have made all the difference in the world.

Questions

1. Do you have a P.O.W.W. network (prayer, other Christians, worship, and the Word) set up for yourself and your family? How can you create a network or strengthen the existing one?

2. How can you more intentionally include eternal moments in your day?

3. What situations in your child's life can you use to teach absolute truth?

Parenting Tips

1. Plan a family Bible study. Be flexible.

2. Investigate programs and activities in which your child participates to be sure the truth is taught.

3. Incorporate messages of faith throughout your home.

PRAYER

Sweet Jesus,

You are the Way and the Truth and the Life. You provide solid ground on which my family can stand. Help me to train my children in biblical truth and steer them away from the lies of the world. Give me opportunities for eternal moments. May my children love and trust Your Word always. Let my legacy of faith be Christ-like.

You alone are the light of the world.

Amen

A SHARED TRUST IN GOD BINDS TOGETHER A FAMILY; WITHOUT IT, WE ARE MORALLY ADRIFT.

Dale Salwak[19]

Section Six

Love Is an Action

Chapter 11

Choose to Protect

Love always protects.

1 Corinthians 13:7a

Protection

Tom and I (Lori) had been parents for less than twenty-four hours and were in a foreign country with a seriously ill baby.

"Maybe our little one has a quiet disposition," we thought. She wouldn't eat, cry, wiggle, or urinate like the babies the other adoptive parents were holding.

She was quiet, very quiet, actually lethargic. Her skin felt clammy. As I held her, she looked up at me with her beautiful big brown eyes. I sensed she trusted us, her mommy and daddy, right from the start.

"Do you think she is okay?" we asked each other.

"What would you do if she was your daughter?" Tom asked Isabel, our Colombian liaison.

"I'd bring her to my cousin." Her cousin was a pediatrician in Bogota. We drove across the city to the clinic.

"Your daughter is severely dehydrated and if you cannot hydrate her, she must be hospitalized." Isabel translated her cousin's diagnosis and warning.

170

The doctor gave us a mixture of water, carrot juice, an empty container, and an eyedropper. Every hour we forced fluid into our child's mouth. We'd fill a twenty-four-ounce jar with the mixture and feed her with the eyedropper. The process took almost an hour each time. This is how we spent our second night as a new family. In the hospital, our babe would have been hydrated intravenously, but the doctor felt it was better for us to treat her at the Hotel Residencia, the inn where we were staying in Colombia. We trusted this doctor and her cousin.

Twenty-four hours later, our daughter found her voice, was able to wet her diaper, and began to squirm a little each time the dropper met her lips. We were so inexperienced we didn't comprehend the seriousness of her condition. But God equips parents with a protective instinct. In spite of being novice parents, we knew it was up to us to keep her well and safe.

Parents are the child's first line of defense for the protection of body, mind, and spirit. We want our kids to be healthy and happy. We do our best to prevent illness and sadness. But in life there are no guarantees things will go well. In fact Jesus says, "In this world you will have trouble. But take heart! I have overcome the world" (John 16:33b). Reality and truth. We want home to be a place that provides secure love. Kids who have their need for security met are able to develop faith, so when life isn't healthy or happy, the knowledge that Christ is the Overcomer still stands. Parents need to protect not hover, love not smother.

David Stark, pastor and LifeKeys co-author, referenced a study during a class Scott and I (Becky) attended. He said that researchers investigated the play habits of elementary children in a fenced and unfenced play area. According to the study, the children used the entire play space as long as the fences around the parameter were in place. When the fences were removed, the children acted insecure and anxious, playing only in the center of the playground. Once the fences were replaced, the children resumed their play using the entire field. Scott and I recall this analogy often as our children mature. Rules and guidelines provide boundaries for children that in turn give them a sense of security. The Lord provides rules for our safety as well. Rules protect.

SAFETY FIRST

I shared a *Denver Post* cartoon with Becky. We both thought it was a good commentary on "extreme" safety. In the illustration four kids were standing on a playground, looking perplexed. The playground didn't have the typical equipment. No swings. No slides. No climbing structures. Instead it had lots of big, rounded plastic shapes with no sharp sides. All the equipment looked to be about three feet high. There was a sign on the playground that read, "Kid-Safe Playground." The caption read, "Remember when playgrounds were fun?"[20]

Typically speaking, moms are more safety conscious than dads. Dads are known as the risk-takers. Children love playing with Dad. Mom may say, "Don't climb any higher. That's high enough. I don't want you to get hurt." Dad is more apt to say, "Let's see how high you can go." Life is more fun when there is a bit of a challenge, a risk. Of course, a calculated or reasonable risk is best. Our kids like a small element of danger. It feels good to be brave and scare Mom just a little! Foolishness is to be avoided, but we don't want our kids to be afraid of their shadow either.

Teaching our kids to protect themselves from harm is common sense. Looking both ways before crossing a street, keeping hands off a hot burner, carrying scissors with the point down are all practices to insist upon and enforce. Safety rules aren't flexible or negotiable.

Car seats, outlet covers, hearth pads, corner guards. Parents do their best to protect their children. Car seats turn into seatbelts. Hearth pads and corner guards are eventually removed. The way safety looks changes as kids age, but it is always a concern.

A nonnegotiable safety issue in my (Becky) family is wearing helmets. The risk of a concrete head-clunking is high with boys that bike, rollerblade, and skateboard. I keep a few extra helmets in the garage for times when "helmetless" friends come to play. Recently, my son's friend showed up without a helmet and ended up wearing mine. He had a bad wipeout that day. I am so thankful the helmet was securely fastened. While I was treating his road rash, both elbows, both knees, and a shoulder injury, he told me how his head hit and bounced off the pavement. My boys and their friends know the rule: no helmet, no wheels.

When it comes to issues of safety, be the Controller. Speak the directive, expect the regulation to be obeyed, and enforce the rule. When a reasonable challenge presents itself, be the Coach and give encouragement with guidance. In this way the elements of security and freedom are both satisfied.

Oh, Nuts!

"How do you protect your child yet give him wings when he has a serious condition?" I (Lori) wrote on my Facebook status. My children have had emergency situations such as broken bones and cuts that need stitches but no issues that are a day-to-day safety concern. Many parents messaged me with their strategies. They had a lot of practical ideas.

"The first eighteen months of my son's life he was ill a lot," one parent wrote. "The doctor suggested he move from milk-based products to almond milk. Lots of kids have dairy issues. He ingested his first cup of the new milk, shortly after he got a runny nose and hives. We didn't connect the dots. Following his second experience with the almond milk we had the paramedics in our home. His tongue swelled; he was having trouble breathing. Thankfully his air supply wasn't totally cut off."

This mom's son has a life-threatening allergy to tree nuts: walnuts, pecans, cashews, pistachios, and almonds. Lots of kids have a peanut allergy, but not as many have a tree nut allergy. The parents now carefully read the ingredient labels on food; ask questions at restaurants; and continually educate teachers, friends, and family about their son's allergy. They are not being overly protective. It is a matter of life and death.

They considered homeschooling and private schools. Fear of not being able to protect their son from an allergic episode loomed. They finally decided upon a local public school. The administration and teachers were willing to partner with them to keep their five-year-old safe. At registration a supply list went out to the parents. Included on the kindergarten form was information about Jack's allergy. The parents rallied as well. They did their best to comply in order to keep the student safe.

Putting the five-year-old into a school was a huge leap of faith for this mom. Between the ages of five and six her son began to be a good self-advocate. He learned to inquire if nuts were in a homemade or store-bought shared treat. "I can't have that," he learned to say.

One of his teachers had him tell the class about his two ambulance rides and close call with death. This was a wise approach. Jack got the support of the other students and looked like a cool guy! Epi-Pens are kept close by, in Dad's car, Mom's purse, and the nurse's office at school.

"How do you handle events like birthday parties and playdates?" I asked.

"We usually have friends come to our home," the mother said. "With birthday parties I still hang out at the party. A time is coming when I won't be able to do that. I know my involvement will become less and less as he gets older."

I asked the parents who responded to my original Facebook question, "What advice would you give moms and dads of children with a life-threatening allergy?" Their recommendations were consistent with this mom's advice:

- ♥ Keep a safe treat at school for celebrations. For example, keep cupcakes in the school freezer when birthdays are celebrated.

- ♥ Educate your child. Teach him to ask questions and avoid foods that will make him sick.

- ♥ Enlist the help of your child's pals.

- ♥ Inform teachers, coaches, and other parents.

- ♥ Anticipate moments like half-time snacks or holidays, and provide alternatives.

In addition, one mom shared this advice given to her by her pediatrician:

Once I knew my son had a peanut allergy, I told the pediatrician my new mission was to educate the school board and administration about trail mix and its dangers. The doctor dissuaded me. "The best thing to do is to educate your son on what he can and can't have," he said. "Teach him to ask questions and avoid foods that will make him sick." This was the best advice I received.

You can't isolate your child. He needs to live in this world. He just needs some special concessions. Empower him to communicate his health issue clearly. This will help lessen the worry when your child has taken ownership of the allergy.

Wise words from a wise mom!

Windows to the Soul

Boundaries need to be created in the areas of spiritual and emotional safety, too. Other families will have views different from your family standards. The idea of taking your little family and moving to a secluded island can sound appealing. Often we feel as though we want to put our kids in the proverbial bubble.

The parents of your child's friends will impact your family. The Chum or Clueless parents may influence your family dynamics in a negative way. Parents who hold a different worldview *will* affect your family. Parental peer pressure is a force to be reckoned with. Refrain from judging other parents. Be true to your values and honor the job God has given you. Avoid the parenting extremes of permissiveness and possessiveness. Seek balanced and appropriate protectiveness.

My (Becky) nephew was invited to a birthday party where the boys were going to be watching a movie that my sister and her husband felt was inappropriate for his age. When my sister R.S.V.P.'d, she respectfully thanked the other mom for the invitation. She said her son would love to join them for dinner but wasn't able to stay for the show. Without casting judgment on the host family, her convictions and actions protected her child.

There is a lot of variety in entertainment. Families have differing guidelines. Deciding what your own family standards are will help determine what is acceptable and unacceptable. Guard your youngster against unwholesome influences.

Discernment for children five and older is an important trait to develop. We want our kids, even the young ones, to understand why something is okay or not, so when they are away from home, they are able to make wise decisions. Media selections are a perfect example. Are your family guidelines clear? If you don't have limits or they are not stated regularly, it's time to begin.

1. Decide how much screen time you will allow (television, computers, games).

2. Discuss family values when watching a show or movie together. Discuss appropriate/ inappropriate content. Talk to him about why you prefer one show over another. Ask your child what he thinks about a commercial or program.

3. Set the standard for appropriate material given your child's age, stage, and personality. Pay attention to your little one's nature. If he's prone to hitting, avoid violent shows or cartoons altogether.

4. Provide your child the words to use to say no to unacceptable entertainment when in someone else's home. "Can we watch something else or play a game instead? I'm not allowed to watch _____."

5. Listen to song lyrics. Determine and discuss appropriateness.

Set the family standard for any type of visual or audio media. Show your child how to identify and avoid unwholesome material. Continue to guide him in discerning good from bad and allow opportunities to make media decisions.

"I will set before my eyes no vile thing" (Psalm 101:3). The eyes are called the window to the soul. We don't want pop culture training our kids. When children are guarded and guided along the way, parents can have more confidence to let them choose and make their own decisions. This will set the stage for success, but it is not a guarantee children will always choose well.

> ### SHOW YOUR CHILD HOW TO IDENTIFY AND AVOID UNWHOLESOME MATERIAL.

PHONE HOME

Playing at a friend's home, having sleepovers, and attending slumber parties are all part of being a kid. To be wise decision-makers parents need to think through some things before an invitation is accepted. Better to be prepared with an answer than caught off guard. Ask yourself:

1. Is my child ready to be away from me for this length of time?

2. What do I think is a good age to spend the night at a friend's house?

3. How well do I know the family?

4. Do I feel comfortable with the family's lifestyle?

5. How often should my child engage in these gatherings?

Get-togethers like this can be fun and provide a small taste of independence. A sound decision will help increase the likelihood of a good experience for the child. If your child feels uncomfortable when away from home, let him know he can call you and you will come and get him.

Neither of my (Lori) two older kids expressed an interest in going to camp. But when my third child was only nine-years-old, she pleaded to go to a five-day camp.

"Please, Mom," she said. "I really want to go. Courtney and Carissa are going. We can be in the same cabin if we sign up together." The three pals had heard about this particular Christian camp in Sunday school.

Nine seemed pretty young to go off to camp. The upside was she would be with two friends. My husband and I knew both families well, so that was a comfort. Church camp, well, that seemed good. The camp was only ninety minutes away from our home. Another positive.

I remembered how I loved being a camper: singing around the campfire, going to chapel, eating in the mess hall, playing games, swimming, and having flashlight devotions in the cabin. It was a terrific experience and a great time of spiritual growth. But I had been four years older than my daughter's nine years.

I hate having her away for a week. She's never been apart from us that long, I thought.

My husband anticipated this separation would be harder on me than her.

We agreed to let her go, paid the fees, and drove her to camp. I was feeling braver as I saw my daughter's excitement grow.

"This will be good," I convinced myself. "If it doesn't look okay, then we don't have to leave her." As this thought popped in my mind, I chose to keep it to myself.

We met the other two families at the camp. The three campers were grinning and jumping with joy. Two of the three moms were hesitant. We brought the girls' sleeping and duffle bags to the cabin. So far so good. Same cabin. Bathrooms were outside the cabin and down the hill. *Hmm. Not so good,* I thought.

We met the counselor, definitely not the warm fuzzy type. My stomach cramped up. The other less-than-enthusiastic mom and I exchanged glances. We were thinking the same thing, *I don't like this….*

Images of my daughter when she was younger flashed in my head. Memories of her calling to come home in the middle of the night from a sleepover flooded my thoughts.

"She's not ready!" my brain screamed.

"She'll be fine," my husband said. He must have read my mind. "All three girls are together."

The next afternoon, three phone calls were placed to three different residences. All three calls originated from the camp. All three homes received the same message: "Your daughter is extremely homesick and needs to go home."

The combination of the three not being totally ready for the adventure and a drill sergeant counselor was not a good mix. Once one girl began to cry the others started, too.

The three moms drove together to collect the three sad campers. Homesickness is highly contagious!

In letting go of the reigns a little, sometimes things don't go as expected. We could have said no from the start, but then our daughter wouldn't have had a small taste of independence. We could have made her stick it out once she was there, but that seemed cruel. Making the best call can be tough. Rest assured, many elementary campers do just fine their first time away from home. Sometimes parenting requires trial and error.

LEARNING CURVE

Take yourself back to a time when you learned something valuable. Most likely it was from a situation not handled well. This is true for kids, too. Removing yourself, letting natural consequences play out, and allowing children to handle trials will strengthen and encourage them to eventually grow into healthy young adults.

In *Psychology Today* Hara Estroff Marino points out parents are actually making their children fragile by not allowing a few scrapes on the playground and opportunities to work through interpersonal issues.

Taking all the discomfort, disappointment and even the play out of development, especially while increasing pressure for success, turns out to be misguided by just about 180 degrees. With few challenges all their own, kids are unable to forge their creative adaptations to the normal vicissitudes of life. That not only makes them risk-averse, it makes them psychologically fragile, riddled with anxiety. In the process they're robbed of identity, meaning and a sense of accomplishment, to say nothing of a shot at real happiness. Forget, too, about perseverance, not simply a moral virtue but a necessary life skill. These turn out to be the spreading psychic fault lines of 21st-century youth. Whether we want to or not, we're on our way to creating a nation of wimps.[21]

Carefully consider when to protect and when to allow nature to take its course. There are circumstances where our children need assistance and support. Determine when to step in by asking these questions: Have I asked my child if he wants or needs help? Have I asked my child how he will resolve the problem?

If the child chooses to take control of a difficult situation, listen to his plan. Ask if he'd like any input. Tom and I experienced a situation where one of our kids was having a conflict with a friend. Our protective instinct kicked in. We wanted to call up that kid's parents and give them a piece of our mind. Thank God we slowed down and asked some Consultant questions: "Do you want help with this? If not, how will you handle this situation?"

It was difficult to have restraint, be only a sounding board, and allow our eight-year-old child to handle it. Stepping back rather than swooping in was the best way to handle this issue. Sometimes an emotional parent can muddy the waters. Often kids can resolve interpersonal conflicts more quickly if the adults back off. Provide wise counsel, and don't hold a grudge. Kids are in the process of learning to navigate social situations. Turn this into a learning opportunity.

Effective Advocate

Parents are called to be their child's advocate in situations outside the home and within the school walls. There are times it is necessary for parents to enter in to help resolve a conflict. Kathy Namura, veteran principal of sixteen years, states the following practical ways to interact when there's a school issue:

Parents must remember that just as no parent sets out to be an ineffective parent, no teacher or principal sets out to be ineffective. Differences may be a matter of perspective. Teachers react most positively to parents who are passionate but not pushy, are involved but not obsessive. Teachers respond to parents who understand that different perspectives can occur and are able to agree to disagree. Teachers appreciate parents who are tactful and non-confrontational in their approach. When there is a concern, approach the teacher with a willingness to listen, then clearly and respectfully state the concern, and ask for the teacher's help in working toward a solution, if there's no resolution go to the principal. Being an effective advocate for your child does not mean defending everything your child does. Avoid the pitfall of assuming the child is always right or truthful. Part of growing up is to assume responsibility for actions, admit mistakes, and accept consequences or accolades for those actions. Children who have learned these lessons are successful in life.[22]

SAFE IN HIS ARMS

We can't always protect our children. Our kids need to know Who can protect them 24/7.

Be proactive in your efforts to keep your child safe. Allow room for error and avoid rescuing. Be respectful by asking your child if he needs assistance when he struggles. Begin to step back bit by bit as your child develops in his skills and character. Let your child grow from dependence on you to dependence on God. Pray Psalm 18:2 for your child. "The LORD is (insert your child's name) rock, his fortress and his deliverer; his God is his rock, in whom he takes refuge, his shield and the horn of his salvation, his stronghold."

> **LET YOUR CHILD GROW FROM DEPENDENCE ON YOU TO DEPENDENCE ON GOD.**

Love Notes on Protection

Lori writes: I think I did a pretty good job training my youngsters to move from dependence on me to interdependence and independence. I wish I'd done a better job training them to be dependent on God. If I had it to do over, I would encourage each child to memorize a Bible verse to call on in times of need.

Becky writes: When my boys were in elementary school, I started praying over them before they left in the morning. This practice has become part of our routine. If I forget, my sons remind me. It comforts me to know the Lord is with each one during the day. I cannot always protect them, but God can.

Questions

1. What safety rules are nonnegotiable in your home?
2. How do you handle issues with a person in authority over your child?
3. What clear family guidelines have you established regarding media content?

Parenting Tips

1. Discuss and enforce media expectations.
2. Teach your child how to be a self-advocate regarding life-threatening allergies.
3. Be tactful and non-confrontational when discussing an issue with your child's teacher.

Prayer

Heavenly Father,

Thank You for Your protection and provisions for my family. You provide security for my family through Your Son, Jesus

Christ. Help me to protect my children spiritually, mentally, emotionally, and physically. May I be respectful of others who parent differently than I do. Fill me with your grace. Assist me in creating boundaries and enforcing the stated expectations. Guide me about when to step in and when to step back.

In Your holy, protective name,

Amen

BUT LET ALL WHO TAKE REFUGE IN YOU BE GLAD;
LET THEM EVER SING FOR JOY.
SPREAD YOUR PROTECTION OVER THEM,
THAT THOSE WHO YOU LOVE YOUR NAME MAY REJOICE IN YOU.

Psalm 5:11

CHAPTER 12

CHOOSE TO TRUST

LOVE ALWAYS TRUSTS.

1 Corinthians 13:7b

DEVELOP TRUST

A mom of a two-and-a-half-year-old wasn't certain whether she should be impressed or concerned about her son's ability to "spin a yarn." When she came home from work, she noticed a large scratch on the coffee table.

"Who did this?" she asked, pointing to the scratch. On a nearby shelf were four metal figurines, each one named and given a distinct personality by her son. They were supposed to be looked at only. The mother deduced her little guy had been playing with them on the table.

"Mahwee did it," he said, not missing a beat. He was blaming Mary, his nanny.

"My husband and I didn't know what to think," the mother said. "Should we be amazed or worried our toddler could cover his tracks so quickly? Do we have an especially astute child or a big schemer on our hands?" the mom wondered.

Maybe the child in the story will turn out to be highly gifted and creative. I don't know. I do know the information contained in this chapter will help parents navigate through situations like this. In the meantime, I'd keep a sharp eye on this kid!

Becky and I will take a close look at trust by exploring different types of lies and how to attack lying by taking into account the child's developmental stage. Parents can learn how to work through the child's feelings of fear, anxiety, worry, and stress and can understand how to encourage security and trust through communication and keeping promises. We have included a special section regarding worries and fears of the gifted child. "Love always trusts" is the outcome of established trustworthy relationships. By developing trust in the home, ultimately our children will learn to trust God.

A Nose Job

Becky and I find it helpful to break down common lies into three categories: attention, acceptance, and avoidance. The liar usually has a reason for the lie, at least at the start. (After a lot of "practice," lying can become habitual.)

Attention lies may look like a fantasy. Often little ones, age six and under, tell these sorts of untruths. There's no need to worry unless this fanciful pattern continues past age seven. When my daughter was three, she had a vivid imagination. She noticed her older siblings, five and seven years of age, were able to do lots of fun things when they were away from home. When we drove past a point of interest, she would say, "I went there with Miss Kathy." This was a complete fabrication. She wasn't being a liar; she was living a little fantasy. Her life wasn't quite as interesting as her siblings. She'd found a remedy, an imaginary life.

If your child engages in this type of storytelling, he's most likely gifted with a great imagination. While listening to his story, help him put it in the proper framework. "Your story about meeting the dinosaur is great. I will write the story down and you can do the illustrations. You have a wonderful imagination." By doing this, the child begins to differentiate between fact and fantasy. He has a proper outlet for his fantasy and receives the attention he's seeking.

Acceptance lies are usually done by children a little older, ages eight and up. These lies are told so their belonging and security needs are met. This is more serious than the usually harmless attention lies. Acceptance lies are done with full knowledge that what's being said is untrue. Kids that tell acceptance lies are often children who think love and inclusion are performance-based. That belief is typically the root of the problem.

If your son or daughter engages in acceptance untruths, then work on affirming the child for who he or she is, encourage character traits you'd like to see develop. Demonstrate unconditional love and acceptance as the long-term solution to the problem. The short-term solution is to catch him in the lie and have him fess up. Insist he restate the truth, acknowledging the lie. Provide understanding and empathy rather than harsh judgment. In humility, share an experience where, as a child, you told a lie to get someone to like you and explain how that was the wrong approach. If the child is seeking a friendship in which he needs to lie to be accepted, then there's a good chance this is a potentially poisonous relationship. The child may have trouble socially and need help with the social nuances of making friends. Put on your Coach's cap and give your child tools to help make friends. Encourage desired friendships by inviting the potential buddy on outings or playdates. Role-play and talk to your child about how to make and be a friend.

If your child is engaged in an acceptance lie, then the best strategy is stating the truth. Confess the lie, apologize, and ask for forgiveness. The response of the person who's been lied to can't be a factor in taking responsibility for the lie. If the acceptance lie has been told to the parent, then know at the heart of the lie is the desire to be loved and accepted.

Deal with the lie; love the child.

Lies of avoidance are done to keep oneself out of trouble. These lies come in two forms: commission and omission. Parents or grandparents may actually be instrumental in instructing children how to lie. Shocking? Yes, but very common.

"What happens at _____ stays at _____," is the worst line. When used like this, "What happens at Grandma's stays at Grandma's," the lie of omission is being promoted. Unintentionally, the grandparent is actually conspiring with the child to keep Mom and Dad in the dark. This puts the child in the unenviable position of being tempted beyond what he can bear. This is flat out wrong! (I don't mince words, sorry.) Lies of omission conveniently leave out the truth. Honesty and fun can go together. Grandparents need to be respectful and abide by the parents' rules if a clear "No" has already been spoken. There may be a time when it is okay to say, "Let's fill Mom and Dad in on our day. Sometimes grandparents do things differently than parents." After all it is called the *Grandparent Prerogative!* A grandparent's actions leave a huge impression on the grandchild. Moms and dads, it is good to lighten up a bit and allow grandparents to have some fun with your child. On the rare occasion, a little ice cream before dinner isn't a big deal. Don't be a spoiler when grandparents want to spoil.

Parents may also be guilty of modeling dishonesty. "Answer that call for me and tell the phone solicitor I'm not here," is a boldfaced lie, a lie of commission. Instead, teach truth. Answer the phone, "I'm not interested. Please take me off your call list. Thank you." Show integrity and strength by dealing directly with the problem.

> ## KIDS THAT TELL ACCEPTANCE LIES ARE OFTEN CHILDREN WHO THINK LOVE AND INCLUSION ARE PERFORMANCE-BASED.

NOT ME!

Parents can unconsciously teach avoidance lies, the untrue statements to keep oneself out of trouble. Here is a common scenario: The child is sitting at the kitchen table, alone. The parent leaves the room momentarily and returns to find the apple juice spilled.

"Who did this?"

The child, reacting to the parent's irritated tone, thinks, *Hmm, if she doesn't know, I'm not telling.* He responds, "I dunno," or "I didn't do it."

Instead, when returning to the kitchen, state, "I see the juice spilled. That's okay. Everybody spills. I'll help you clean it up."

While cleaning up, discuss the fact that everyone spills and accidents happen. During the conversation ask the child, "What would be a way to avoid spilling your juice?"

Note the balance of the Chum and Consultant strategies in this scene. The child has an opportunity to tell the truth in a nonthreatening environment and has a chance to think about spillage and accident prevention while feeling loved and understood by Mom or Dad. An added blessing is the grace your child experiences in your home.

This nonthreatening approach could have worked well for the parents in the story about the scratched table in the previous section. Rather than asking who did it, state what you see, how it can be fixed, and what you think happened. "I see a scratch on the table. I know you love those metal characters. Looks like you were playing with them on the table. I think we can rub the scratch out. You can help me. How can this be avoided in the future?" Speaking these words will help your child ease into confession. Admitting wrongdoing and saying he's sorry for the scratch is going to be less scary. "Whoever conceals their sins does not prosper, but the one who confesses and renounces them finds mercy" (Proverbs 28:13).

> ## PARENTS CAN UNCONSCIOUSLY TEACH AVOIDANCE LIES.

TAKE THE HIT

Deflecting responsibility is a form of the avoidance lie. The one being accused quickly turns the tables so the responsibility of the action is another's to bear. A common scene in the home was described by a mom in Becky's parenting class.

"I heard crying," the mom said. "I had just left the playroom to toss a load of laundry into the washer. I ran back to my children to see what was wrong. My tear-drenched, two-year-old daughter was holding her head. I noticed my composed four-year-old was holding a plastic hammer."

"You *hitted* me with that," the two-year-old wailed.

"I did not," the four-year-old said. "You got in my way." Clever twist.

The mother wondered, "How can my child lie to my face while holding the 'weapon'?"

Answer, he can with no problem. He comes by it naturally, a version of self-preservation. Just like in the Garden of Eden (Genesis 3). When the Lord questioned Adam as to why he ate the forbidden fruit, he blamed Eve, and then faulted God. God did in fact make that woman! The finger pointing continued with Eve blaming the serpent. Neither took responsibility for their actions. This pattern continues today.

When your three-year-old begins to fib by deflecting or claiming innocence, there is no cause for alarm, but there is cause for action. At three, the youngster has discovered parents are not mind readers. As the child gets a little older, between ages four and six, he becomes more proficient at telling untruths. By the time a child is in elementary school he has become quite convincing and sophisticated. This is a behavior to squelch. Don't call your child a liar but do expect him to confess. Discuss the importance of honesty. This is an ongoing process and worth the effort.

GO TO THE SOURCE

Open communication with our kids is a great way to establish and reinforce trust. When my (Becky) son was in first grade, an older student took it upon himself to teach him "the birds and the bees" on the playground. My son came home with an anatomically correct definition of sex. Because he was open with us and told us what he had learned, Scott and I had an opportunity to sit down with him and have an age-appropriate discussion of how God has blessed mommies and daddies with a special loving way to have babies.

When he asked if we ever did "that," we pointed to him. He shut his eyes, crinkled up his nose, and said, "Gross!"

My husband and I have worked on keeping the lines of communication open. Now that our son is older, the discussions regarding sex include how to treat a young woman with respect, the detriments of pornography, and the goal of purity through abstinence. We want him to hear from us how to view sex, not from a pal on the playground.

When trust is established between parent and child, the child is more apt to seek the parent to verify information. By staying cool and not freaking out when asked about sexual things, the likelihood of your child checking with you about interesting facts gleaned from peers will increase.

> **WHEN TRUST IS ESTABLISHED BETWEEN PARENT AND CHILD, THE CHILD IS MORE APT TO SEEK THE PARENT TO VERIFY INFORMATION.**

PROMISE KEEPER

Kids learn to be true to their word by observing their parents. Build a foundation of honesty by meaning what you say and saying what you mean. "Simply let your 'Yes' be 'Yes,' and your 'No,' 'No'" (Matthew 5:37a). Values and morals are best taught by example. Stand by your word. Be worthy of your child's trust. If you've promised to take your child somewhere, then make good on your promise. If you've said you'll listen to his story when you're done cooking, then follow through. If your child says, "I know you'll forget to toss the football with me," then you can be certain a parental pattern of not carrying out a promise is being established and the child has noticed. Your son or daughter's faith and trust in you is slowly depleting. Being a promise keeper builds trust.

Sticking to the facts makes a parent trustworthy, too. Exaggerating and embellishing stories teaches children to lie. We tell lies that seem so trivial so as not to hurt someone's feelings or to save face. Usually a lie has a component of fear, fear of rejection or fear of being found out. Author Cecil Murphey states, "Jesus wouldn't lie for any reason. He might wisely choose to remain silent, but he had nothing to hide and nothing to protect. Maybe that's the big difference: we still have things to protect."[23]

> **IF YOU'VE PROMISED TO TAKE YOUR CHILD SOMEWHERE, THEN MAKE GOOD ON YOUR PROMISE.**

365 TIMES

"Do not be afraid." Three hundred sixty-five times this statement is written in Scripture. No fear for every day of the year. Fear, anxiety, and worry plague adults. These emotions can be debilitating and problematic for kids, too. Young children have a limited amount of understanding, no depth of experience, and a vivid imagination. When kids are scared, they are scared big time. And it is real.

Infants and toddlers typically fear loud noises, new faces, and separation from parents. Being afraid of the dark, monsters, and storms are common among preschoolers. School-aged children are concerned about death, natural disasters, and real or imagined issues at school.

There are some things adults can do to lessen a child's fear factor. By avoiding negative methods of parenting, such as threats when you are angry, harsh punishment, and unattainable expectations, a child's propensity for being fearful will be reduced. Overprotectiveness can also be the cause of a fearful and timid child. These are all high controlling behaviors, the Controller style at its worst.

Fears can be real or imagined. And some fear can be a friend. Healthy fear prevents children from touching a hot stove. Unhealthy, imagined, or excessive fear can paralyze a child from participating in normal activity. Fear in the wrong context can be a foe.

When my kids were young, we lived in San Diego. Fleas, cockroaches, tarantulas, and termites are common in that part of the country. Mosquitos are not. When we first arrived at my parents' home in Minnesota for a family summer vacation, my son got a flavor of the great outdoors—Minnesota style.

As the sun began to lower my mom said, "We'd better go inside. The mosquitoes are coming out."

My almost-three-year-old son made a beeline for the house at warp speed. If Nana said to go in, he was going in. Mosquitoes must be really scary! His limited amount of experience regarding the "Minnesota state bird" caused him to be fearful.

SCARE TACTICS

A vivid imagination without life experience produces fear as well. Kids under seven have many fears. Clowns, Santa, and big stuffed animals that walk and talk are creepy to some youngsters. Tom and I had to tell Goofy to go away so we could get our terrified daughter out from under a table. Don't force your child to embrace these characters. So what if your little one doesn't shake Mickey's hand at Disneyland or sit on Santa's lap? Forcing your child into a fearful situation, ridiculing him about his fear, or ignoring the fear will encourage its growth rather than removal. Instead, give your child reassurance, limited exposure to the feared object, and help him find a way to understand new things.

When our children are afraid, the best response is to keep calm, explain the situation, and gently move on. Explain that fear is an emotion God gives us to keep us safe. Discuss things that are wise to fear. Living in Colorado, my family knew a rattlesnake on the trail is wise to fear. (One even bit my dog, nasty thing!) But observing a rattlesnake in a glass cage at the zoo isn't scary.

Fears can be transferred, too. If you scream at the sight of a spider, the child will most likely become afraid of those eight-legged creatures. Be aware of your own fears; don't pass them along to your child.

Identify healthy and imagined fears. Make a plan to deal with the fear. Is your young one afraid of the dark? Get a nightlight, and keep the closet door shut. Be sensitive, listen, and reassure your child. Teach him how to pray an arrow prayer when afraid: "God, I'm really scared of _____ right now. Help me to remember you are bigger and stronger than anything that might frighten me. Give me peace." Remind your child of the words of Philippians 4:5b: "The Lord is near," so we don't need to fear.

> ### THE LORD IS NEAR, SO WE DON'T NEED TO FEAR.

HUG 'N' GO

I (Lori) received an e-mail asking how to deal with separation anxiety in a four-year-old. The little guy was having trouble leaving Mom's side when going to preschool. Previously he hadn't had any trouble and the mom was concerned. As more information came to light, I could understand the situation.

Her son had just recovered from the flu. His schedule had been interrupted by the illness. It's not unusual for a child to suddenly develop separation anxiety after an injury or illness. Being with Mom or Dad when not feeling up to par satisfies the child's basic need for security.

When your child is having separation issues, act confident about the circumstances. "You are going to school now," you can say. "I will pick you up after lunch." Then give your child a big ol' hug and go. You may need to peel him off of you, but remain calm. Tell yourself, "He will be just fine. I'm leaving him in capable hands." Make certain you arrive to pick him up at the time you said.

The biggest mistake a parent makes is to hang around until things get better. Slipping out when they appear to improve will reinforce the child's insecurity. There are two other reasons hanging around and then slipping out is not good. The child knows he has just manipulated you and it prolongs the child's emotional angst.

One of Becky's boys was very apprehensive the first day of kindergarten. Having a new teacher, riding the bus with big kids, being away from home were all weighing heavily on his mind. To reassure him, Becky drew a small red heart with "XO" on the palm of his hand. "Each time you look at the heart, remember how much I love you." A little love from home goes a long way!

Here are a few additional ideas to help quell separation anxiety.

1. Pray for a smooth transition for yourself and your child.0Pray for a smooth transition for yourself and your child.

2. Visit the school prior to the first day. Check out the playground.

3. Meet the teacher(s) before school starts.

4. Give your child something small and scented to keep in his locker or cubby. Send a photograph of your family in a plastic bag.

5. Every day say, "I love you. I'll always come back for you." Be on time to pick up or greet your child.

6. Arrange for a playdate outside of school to encourage new friendships.

Starting school is hard on child and parent. These ideas should help both!

It's a Gift

Gifted kids can have their own set of fears. These fears revolve around big problems they believe they are born to solve. One gifted six-year-old boy thought it was his job to solve major environmental issues. A seven-year-old girl felt it was her sole responsibility to save the butterflies. Both obsessed over their "calling."

When a child is on a mission, spurred on by fear or concern, allow him to discuss his ideas within workable time constraints. Give enough time to help him feel validated but not so much that he dominates the entire evening. This talk needs to be done only with parents. The child must be told that his peers are not interested in this passion. Often a gifted child will repel other kids due to his obsession. Give the child a notebook to jot down ideas. The passion will eventually peter out, possibly replaced by another worldly concern.

As a side note, the gifted child should have a limited number of choices during the day. If he needs to think through and make choices about everything, then he will quickly lose confidence and trust in his parents. This will feed his fear of having sole responsibility to solve big problems. He will believe he is the only guy with all the answers. Later this will transfer to a lack of respect for authority and a lack of confidence in the "experts," resulting in a stressed out or rebellious child.

Stressed Out

Kindergarten and early elementary school can be stressful times. You may see behaviors you think are disgusting and would like to extinguish. Nose picking, genital grabbing, throat clearing, blinking, and nail biting can be the result of anxiety. The behaviors that are more tic-like (throat clearing, blinking) can be left alone. If you attempt to get rid of a tic, then something bigger may replace it. My (Lori) son chewed his shirt when he was nervous. His collar was always wet and frayed. Most of his t-shirts were ruined. Eventually the need to release stress in this way went away.

The habits of crotch grabbing and nose picking are harder to ignore. Many kids do this, no cause for alarm, but there is less social tolerance for these actions. Especially if the child is age five or older, help your youngster find another outlet for his anxiousness. Encourage your child to verbalize his concerns. Don't nag or punish the child. Try to discover the reason for the anxiety. Be supportive of your young child's efforts to stop the behavior. Pray for peace and confidence to replace anxiety. "Do not be anxious about anything, but in everything, by prayer and petition, with thanksgiving, present your requests to God" (Philippians 4:6).

> ### PRAY FOR PEACE AND CONFIDENCE TO REPLACE ANXIETY.

PENNIES FROM HEAVEN

Trust as a loving component in our families is critical. Trusting in God, crucial. Every day we see coins inscribed with the motto "In God we trust." Most people don't give a penny a second look. It's hardly worth bending over to retrieve. A woman I (Lori) know values pennies. Every time she sees one she picks it up. A few years ago, she lost her son following routine surgery. Rather than cling to the despair, this mom has chosen to hang on to trust.

The penny may only be one cent, but its message is priceless. Give your five- to nine-year-old a penny to put into his pocket, so when he feels fearful, worried, or anxious, he is reminded to trust God. "Trust in the LORD with all your heart and lean not on your own understanding" (Proverbs 3:5).

LOVE NOTES ON TRUST

LORI WRITES: Training my kids to be honest really keeps me honest. Honesty is simple, but it isn't always convenient.

There have been times it would have been easier to keep an item the cashier forgot to ring up rather than go back and pay. But the example of honesty and my integrity are worth more than a blip in my schedule.

BECKY WRITES: When my boys were little, I was so taken with how trusting they were. They would jump into a pool if I was already in the water waiting, try a new food if I said it tasted good, or take medicine if I told them it would make them feel better. I quickly learned if I wanted to keep that sense of trust, I had to be honest and trustworthy.

QUESTIONS

1. What type of lie does your child typically tell (acceptance, attention, or avoidance)? Knowing its type, how can you encourage honesty?

2. What does your child fear? What plan have you put into place to deal with his fear?

3. How can you encourage your child to trust in God when he is afraid?

PARENTING TIPS

1. Help your child distinguish between fact and fantasy.

2. Encourage your child when he has demonstrated honesty.

3. Teach your child how to pray an arrow prayer when afraid.

PRAYER

Heavenly Father,

I desire to be a trustworthy person. Let my lips speak words that are truthful and filled with love. Give me the ability to be a promise keeper. Bless my relationship with my children with honest, open, and loving communication. Strengthen me to trust You in all areas of my life. Present opportunities

for me to show my children how to trust You in good times and hard times. Give me courage to conquer irrational fears. Give me tenderness to deal with my children when they are afraid. Make me bold and courageous for You.
Amen

THOSE WHO KNOW YOUR NAME TRUST IN YOU, FOR YOU, LORD, HAVE NEVER FORSAKEN THOSE WHO SEEK YOU.

Psalm 9:10

SECTION SEVEN

LOVE IS A COMMITMENT

Chapter 13

Choose to Hope

Love always hopes.

1 Corinthians 13:7c

Eyes Forward

When one of my (Becky's) sons was younger, he was notorious for running full tilt, glancing back over his shoulder to see how far he'd run. While looking back at me, his distance marker, he would usually wipe out. As a result, "Look where you're going, not where you've been," has become a Danielson family mantra.

This statement has come in handy as my boys have grown. Focusing on the future rather than the past is helpful and hopeful. Hope keeps us looking and moving forward. Since God is trustworthy and faithful we can have hope.

But Lori and I know it's hard to be hopeful when you feel alone. Hopelessness arrives in the storms of life. The problem lies in the suffering. No one appreciates sleepless nights, knots in the stomach, or feeling impending doom when facing tough situations.

Kids look to parents for encouragement and hope. Parents must be hopeful to have hope-filled kids. Trusting in God's plan as opposed to being defeated in present circumstances or mired in the past is being hopeful.

We'll examine how to experience and encourage hope in times of grief, disappointment, and depression. We'll look at learning disabilities in kids and the role of the parent as the child's advocate. Parents can bring a zest for life back into the family by introducing new or out-of-the-box activities in which to participate. Hope is a gift from God. "Do not let your hearts be troubled. Trust in God; trust also in me" (John 14:1).

> ## LOOK WHERE YOU'RE GOING,
> ## NOT WHERE YOU'VE BEEN.

A PARENT'S DREAM

Remember waiting to see if the "stick would turn blue"? When witnessing the white-to-blue transformation at our home, Scott and I were ecstatic. We called our parents at six o'clock in the morning and started planning our family's future over breakfast!

Hope-filled dreams for a child's future begin at conception. A friend of mine recently gave birth to a beautiful baby girl. The happy parents sent Psalm 126:3 along with pictures in an e-mail. "The LORD has done great things for us, and we are filled with joy." How joyful and hopeful they are as they embark on the parenting journey.

But what if hopes are dashed and dreams die? When a child is born with a deformity, disability, diagnosed with a learning disorder, or is suddenly dealing with a mental illness, hopes and dreams are in need of change. Change is hard. Attitudes matter. Life may not be as we envisioned. Even though it will not be easy, with God's strength it will be okay.

A friend with a child diagnosed with Asperger syndrome is on a mission. Due to her child's disability, her passion has become assisting the school in providing alternative lessons and styles of teaching to meet the needs of her son and other kids. Pictures are a means by which many students comprehend and retain information, so she is helping to revamp the curriculum. Her goal is to help her son and other children to become confident, productive learners in the classroom setting. She is fostering hope.

Special-needs children dealing with physical, mental, or emotional challenges require attention and redefined expectations. Lori and I encourage parents to become students of their child to determine what works. In our parenting classes we discuss breaking tasks and teachings into smaller pieces. We encourage moms and dads to try different modes, such as visual (pictures), tactile (touch), auditory (listening), repetition, memorization, or even musical lyrics to reinforce mastery of a new skill. Music, riddles, stories, and jokes use both left and right brain functions, making them powerful learning tools. Be creative. Use these strategies to help your child learn. *You* are the expert on your child and his best advocate. Research his disability. Seek out other parents who have children with the same issues for support and further information.

Parents of special-needs kids have unique concerns. A special-needs child may put a strain on the parents' marriage, other children, work, finances, personal relationships, and responsibilities. Parents may have to shift much of their time and money toward providing treatment and interventions for the special-needs child.

Here are some helpful tips:

1. Inform your other children about their sibling's challenges.

2. Give your kids a heart for the special-needs child's struggle.

3. Initiate contact with support people (teachers, pastors) and provide information.

4. Set aside time and resources for each child. The focus must not be all on one kid.

5. Be honest about the struggle. Listen to the siblings' point of view.

6. Spend time alone with your spouse to keep the family unit strong.

Veteran principal Kathy Namura has this to say to parents of disabled or special-needs students:

It's especially important to be an advocate if you have a child with special needs. Law requires many of the educational processes that take place when you have a child with special needs. The steps can be daunting! Various people will test your child to gain a total picture of his educational, psychological, social, emotional, and physical abilities as well as the parent's perspective of the child. In meeting school personnel to hear the summarized reports, it may appear very negative; there may be lots of focus on what is "wrong" with the child. Take a deep breath. Realize there needs to be a clear understanding of your child's issues in order to come up with the best possible educational plan and positive approach. As a parent, remember you are very important as a member of the team to educate your child. Willingly give suggestions and honest input and feedback for your child. Have high yet attainable expectations for your child to achieve. The child with special needs may need more organizational help and parental support with schoolwork. Be loving and patient, your child may learn on a different timetable than other children but he will learn.[24]

> A PARENT'S JOB IS TO REMAIN LOVING AND PATIENT, REMEMBERING YOUR CHILD'S TIMETABLE MAY BE A DIFFERENT TIMETABLE, BUT HE WILL LEARN.

I Believe

Hope reintroduces resiliency to life. In times of real or perceived loss while redefining a child's abilities, hope reminds us every day, every hour, every minute of what we believe. Dr. H. Norman Wright says, "Resilient people have a creed that says, 'I believe!' and they affirm that creed daily. In essence they say:

♥ I believe God's promises are true.

♥ I believe heaven is real.

♥ I believe God will see me through.

♥ I believe nothing can separate us from God's love.

♥ I believe God has work for me to do."[25]

In our weakness God reveals His strength, giving us the courage to forge ahead.

"Brothers, we do not want you to be ignorant about those who fall asleep, or to grieve like the rest of men, who have no hope" (1 Thessalonians 4:13). Know what you know. Share it with your child.

Broken Hearts

My (Lori) friend Danielle described her son's birth and his diagnosis. "In the space of two hours I went from heaven to hell," she said. Her newborn had a defect known as hypoplastic left heart syndrome. His little heart wasn't strong enough to pump oxygen through his body.

With hope, he was put on a ventilator following an angioplasty. His name was on the heart transplant list. The parents wanted to give their baby every chance for life they could. As his condition worsened, they opted for a high-risk surgery three days following his birth. They cried. They prayed, "Lord, please let Aidan live so he can share You with others."

Minutes later, the little boy who had so stubbornly fought for his life lost the battle in the operating room.

Danielle recalled, "As I held his lifeless body, my motherly instincts kicked in. I kissed him, spoke to him, rocked him, sang to him. I whispered, 'I love you.' I was caught up in the love and peace of the moment. Then the reality and finality of death came upon me. I screamed at God, 'Why would you create a baby to live for such a short period of time?'

"I challenged God with my questions," Danielle said. "I wondered, 'Are you a God who causes pain? Are you a God who is punishing me for some past sin? Is this some sick lesson on becoming a stronger person?' If the answer was yes, I was no longer interested in this God, the God in whom I placed my trust and committed life."

A month passed and the Lord began to gently remind Danielle who He was. Even though anger was still present, she began to read God's promises in the Bible. She felt Him wrap His loving arms around her as she railed against Him. She felt Him weep when she wept. He walked with her through the valley of the shadow of death. The Father tenderly spoke, "I, too, know the pain of losing my Son. I am here to sit with you in your grief and remind you of my love."

The knowledge of who God is began to return and fill her with hope. To have hope, that knowledge is critical. Knowledge builds trust; trust generates hope. Without clear understanding, we interpret our circumstances through emotion.

Danielle made a choice. She told God, "I choose You. I don't get it, but I choose You."

She and her husband made other choices, too. They knew fifty percent of marriages don't survive the death of a child. They decided to be a part of the half that makes it. They made a pact. Every night they said three positive things about the day, even if the things were as simple as, "The sun is shining."

They gave each other room to grieve. When one was "stinky," as they called it, they chose not to engage in an argument but to attribute the bad attitude to grief.

Crappy things happen. God redeems them. We can choose to get up and keep walking. Hope is a deliberate decision to get out of bed, say three positive things, and to give grace. Hope brings courage.

Danielle and David had a casting made of Aidan's hands and feet, a practice they continued with all their children. Even in his short life Aiden has had an impact on what would be his four younger siblings. Danielle, David, and their four children have learned the value of being the hands and feet of Jesus, serving or sitting with those in need either emotionally, physically, or spiritually. They are hope bringers, offering the hope of God's love and redemption.

Why did God create Aidan to live only three days? Marshall Shelley, a father who has lost two children, says, "He didn't. God created Aidan for eternity."

Hope Bearers

Bringing hope to a broken world means spreading the light of Jesus. Even a small glimmer of hope can dispel darkness. One mom told this story about her eight-year-old daughter. A teacher in her daughter's school had lost a child. This little girl knew of the death and was moved by the grief in the teacher's eyes. She walked up to him one day and said, "I'm sorry about your son. If you need a hug to feel better, I can help you." He welcomed her hug. It was a heartfelt gift of love and compassion.

Young children are so filled with hope. They have a knack for looking on the bright side. Just like the sun illuminates the earth, a kind word or deed can break through the sadness. A note to a friend whose parents have separated, cookies for a classmate recovering from surgery, an offer to help weed the garden of an infirmed neighbor are ways children can reach out. Unselfish acts provide hope. Encourage the next generation to respond as their "brother's keeper," being a support and comfort, just like Jesus.

Vicarious Living

Dashed dreams may come in the form of various disabilities or even a different life vision. Parental hopes and dreams can be miles from the kids' hopes and dreams. There are many parents who live vicariously through their children. Ask yourself these questions: "Is my child passionate about this activity or is he taking part to please me? Who is getting more out of this activity, my child or me?"

My (Becky) brother-in-law was a hockey star in high school and college. He still loves the game. When his oldest son was old enough to skate, he had him on the ice, learning stick handling. His son played hockey for a number of years but disliked the late night and early morning ice times. He had little opportunity to be with his friends and often did his homework in the car. Family time was spent at tournaments. When the son expressed a desire to quit, his dad wisely allowed him to do so. They both still really enjoy NHL games and like to play pick-up games, but the pressure is off. My brother-in-law did not have a need to live his life vicariously through his son. This is a gift to a child.

Admittedly, my husband and I (Lori) did not handle a similar circumstance as well. Our son loved football. We loved watching him play. He was good at it. For many years prior to the first contact practice, our son would talk about quitting the team. His anxiety was elevated in anticipation of that first hit-and-tackle practice. Since he normally carried the ball, he was the target to bring down. Once that first hard-hitting practice was over, his nerves settled down.

When he was thirteen, he announced, "I don't want to play football next year."

His dad and I had heard that before and brushed off his declaration. The following season rolled around. We signed him up. He was unhappy. We'd seen this before.

"I told you," he said. "I don't want to play."

In negative Controller fashion, I continued to haul him to practice. It was miserable getting him into the car to go and then out of the car to the field. He dug his heels in. He didn't have a choice in going, but he sure had a choice in how he was going to play. He chose to play badly.

We'd made a big mistake. Our son's passion for the sport was gone and we hadn't recognized it. We'd relied on a previous behavior pattern and hadn't made note of a lack of zeal for the game. We assumed his football interests would remain the same as always. We were wrong. If we'd listened more closely and asked better questions, we would have been in a position to accurately assess the shift and make changes accordingly.

HOPELESSNESS

Situation and personality play into how your youngster views life. If your child is pessimistic, start training him to see the glass half full. When he loses the soccer game, step in as the Coach and point out the good defense techniques he used. When he gets a low score on a test, as the Consultant, help him to brainstorm ways he can improve his grades. You don't need to be a Pollyanna, but looking for the good fosters optimism and a sense of hope.

Depression and discouragement are emotions children have when they feel as if they are unable to resolve a problem or when they are unable to learn something new. Life feels like an impossible undertaking.

Dr. H. Norman Wright describes seven signs of depression in a child:[26]

1. Appearance: looks sad, depressed, unhappy

2. Withdrawal: shows limited interest in activities, listless; seems ill (headaches, stomach aches, sleeping, eating disturbances)

3. Discontent: gives impression of being dissatisfied, shows little pleasure in what he or she does

4. Rejection: child feels unloved, worthless

5. Irritability: exhibits low tolerance in frustrating situations

6. Provocative: acts out, opposite of being depressed

7. Expressive: expresses depression as rebellion, negativity, anger, or resentment

Dr. Wright goes on to say that depression may be caused by death, divorce, moving, economic issues, parental favoring of a sibling, lack of affection, illness, or a lack of positive feedback for accomplishments.[27]

If depression is grief-related, then accept depression as a normal reaction. Give the child time to adjust. (If the depression is severe, get professional help.) Dr. Wright recommends this: "Let the child know that everyone experiences sadness and depression at one time or another. Be sure to put your explanation into terminology the child can handle. Explain that feelings like this are normal and that in time they will pass and the child will feel better. Let the child know God understands his or her down times as well as happy times."[28]

How do we support our children when they are displaying an attitude of hopelessness and chronic unhappiness? Be hopeful. We are the first line of defense in providing a listening ear, encouragement, and hope for our children. Listen without judging or trying to solve the problem. Often the youngster arrives at a solution while thrashing out the details of the issue at hand. If your child desires help, then put on your Consultant's or Coach's hat to assist in solving the problem. Empathize and lend support. Provide opportunities for your child to develop new interests or experience success. Alter the child's routine to keep things new and exciting. Bring back that zest for life. Spend time together. These things can help your child recover from a state of depression or discouragement.

When the storm's over, we see God's provision, which we often overlook in our angst. "We also rejoice in our sufferings, because we know that suffering produces perseverance; perseverance, character; and character, hope. And hope does not disappoint us, because God has poured out his love into our hearts by the Holy Spirit, whom he has given us" (Romans 5:3b-5). Genesis 9:13 says that the rainbow after a storm is a promise of hope.

PERSONALITY PLAYS INTO ATTITUDES, BUT PARENTAL GUIDANCE CAN GO A LONG WAY IN FOSTERING HOPEFULNESS.

Out-of-the-Box

My youngest son and I (Becky) had planned a special day together. The previous week his older brother had a day off of school due to a teacher workshop. He and I spent the day at the Mall of America's indoor amusement park. We rode the rides and had lunch at his favorite restaurant. My youngest son was really looking forward to his turn. The day his teachers' workshop day arrived so did a foot of snow. School was closed, the teacher workshop was cancelled, and so were our plans.

When he heard about the closures on the news, my fourth-grader was really disappointed. "Why me?" he moaned. "The only snow day we've ever had is on my special day!"

We made the best of the day, spending time together playing in the snowdrifts and baking cookies. But this day did not compare to his older brother's time, so he was still bummed. I'm sure the teachers were saddened, too. The workshop day wasn't rescheduled. Without an alternative day, I hatched a plan.

The following week I surprised my son at breakfast, saying, "Work hard at school this morning. I have a surprise for you this afternoon."

Even with all the questions and pleading, I kept quiet. "Just wait and see," was my only response. Excitement and hope filled his eyes. He loved surprises.

I picked him up just before lunch and signed him out of school for the rest of the day. The two of us had a great time together. He knew this was out-of–the-box behavior for me, a former first-grade teacher. Years later he still talks about our special afternoon. Playing hooky was not only Mom-sanctioned but Mom-instigated. What a great memory!

Out-of-the-box activities with your child are good ways to promote hopefulness. Hope is a confidence that the ones you love will come to the rescue even if the villain is a snowy day.

Look Up

God is the true essence of love and our hope provider. The outcome may not always be what we desire, but God is always faithful. "Be still, and know that I am God," states the psalmist (Psalm 46:10a).

Be still and watch how the Lord provides. Be still and know that God is sovereign, powerful, and mighty even if we are disappointed. Trust.

Oswald Chambers wrote this about hope in *My Utmost for His Highest*, "If our hopes are being disappointed just now, it means that they are being purified. There is nothing noble the human mind has ever hoped for or dreamed of that will not be fulfilled. One of the greatest strains in life is the strain of waiting for God."[29]

With Christ we can hope in something bigger than ourselves. We can be confident of the same hope and instill that confidence in our children. Provide hope by supporting and encouraging your kids in their endeavors. Live with the knowledge that God will always be with you, even in the valleys, filling you with His peace. "May the God of hope fill you with all joy and peace as you trust in him, so that you may overflow with hope by the power of the Holy Spirit" (Romans 15:13).

What a hope we have in Jesus Christ! Without Him we are condemned men and women who cannot save ourselves no matter what we do. We are without hope. With Him, we have the promise of eternal life. "But when the kindness and love of God our Savior appeared, he saved us, not because of righteous things we had done, but because of his mercy. He saved us through the washing of rebirth and renewal by the Holy Spirit, whom he poured out on us generously through Jesus Christ our Savior, so that, having been justified by his grace, we might become heirs having the hope of eternal life" (Titus 3:4-7). A family focused on Christ with a hopeful attitude will tenaciously withstand storms and will flourish.

LOVE NOTES ON HOPE

LORI WRITES: Conjuring up hope by only having a good attitude is impossible. Hope is a supernatural experience. When I'm feeling down in the dumps and having trouble getting out of bed, I pray for God's strength and vision. By putting one foot in front of the other and remembering my God is bigger than the storm and His ways are not my ways, I am able to keep on keeping on with hopeful expectations— one moment at a time.

BECKY WRITES: I have found three ways to reclaim hope in tough circumstances. First, I focus on Scripture to remind myself of the hope I have in Jesus. Second, I share my burdens with God. And third, I help someone in a more difficult spot. I encourage my boys to do the same when they feel hopeless.

QUESTIONS

1. Are your hopes for your child in line with his/her desires and dreams?

2. How do you model hopefulness in a difficult situation?

3. What can you do to bring hope to another in a seemingly hopeless situation?

PARENTING TIPS

1. Encourage kids to look where they're going, not where they've been.

2. Expect compassion from siblings of a special-needs child.

3. Use Dr. Wright's "I believe" creed to help build resiliency in your child.

PRAYER

Heavenly Father,

You are the true essence of hope. Lord, show me how to point my family to You in the midst of the trials or suffering. You are the light, the beacon of hope, an anchor for my soul. May I always reach for You in my despair, knowing You will stoop down and pull me up out of the miry clay. Help me to listen and provide encouragement to my child when he feels hopeless. Stir a desire in me to pray for those in need of hope in their circumstances. Thank You for the hope You give to me, my family, and to the world through Your Son, Jesus.

Amen

WHY ARE YOU DOWNCAST, O MY SOUL?
WHY SO DISTURBED WITHIN ME?
PUT YOUR HOPE IN GOD,
FOR I WILL YET PRAISE HIM, MY SAVIOR AND MY GOD.

Psalm 42:5

Chapter 14

Choose Tenacity

Love always perseveres.

1 Corinthians 13:7d

Against All Odds

"Her condition is called aphasia," the speech clinician said.

The clinician went on to describe the disorder to Tom and me. She said our three-year-old would not succeed in reading, mathematics, and written or verbal communication. She predicted our daughter wouldn't be able to attend regular school or hold a job.

Well, let me tell you, that wasn't our plan and it wasn't God's plan. The Lord gave us supernatural strength and gave tenacity to our child. The clinician's every prediction was false. Either her diagnosis was incorrect or God gave us a miracle. Either way our youngster was speech- and language-delayed, not aphasic. Learning just took a little more time. We all worked together with hopeful determination. She went to regular public school, graduated from high school, attends a local college, and has held a part-time job for more than two years. We have an amazing kid and an *awesome* God! We truly believe "nothing is impossible with God" (Luke 1:37).

Overcoming adversity is an overriding theme throughout Scripture. Genesis through Revelation, God rescues His people from insurmountable odds: He parted the Red Sea for the Israelites, protected

Daniel in the lion's den, and gave David strength to slay Goliath (Exodus 14, Daniel 6, 1 Samuel 17). Reading biblical accounts to children gives them the facts about the ability of God to do mighty things. Hope, humongous and contagious hope, provides the motivation to be tenacious. Hope is the strong will or desire to push through toward a specific goal.

If we understand how our children learn, then we are better equipped to support them. Parents in our classes express the desire to have their children embrace a healthy work ethic, the ability to persevere when the "goin' gets tough," and an understanding that everyone struggles with something. Not having a critical spirit ourselves fosters a willing spirit in our children.

Life is filled with challenges and victories. Many life struggles bring about suffering. In this chapter, Becky and I present ways to care for youngsters in the midst of hard times.

James 5:11 says, "As you know, we consider blessed those who have persevered. You have heard of Job's perseverance and have seen what the Lord finally brought about. The Lord is full of compassion and mercy." Tenacity is a godly trait.

CRITICAL EYE OR CRITICAL I

The idea of having a critical eye is good. It helps us discern what way is best. But a critical spirit is a negative nature, picking out and picking at things that need improvement. It is adversarial and overbearing.

Parents want their children to succeed and notice when they don't. Moms and dads with a critical eye have a choice. Correct or criticize. Becky and I endorse correction done with affirming words to motivate kids to try again. This type of correction shows love and concern. Criticism, on the other hand, attacks the person. It either provides zero direction or dictates the entire process. Critical observations make children feel inadequate. (They make me feel inadequate, too!) For kids to feel capable, nurturing a positive self-image through gentle correction mixed with a you-can-do-it attitude is critical. Continued criticism causes frustration, anger, and actually encourages a resentful or quitter mentality.

Parents are the ones to prepare the way for the child's learning. When kids face a difficult task, use encouragement to foster tenacity, set goals to build determination, and provide hope to increase resiliency. If your parental comments are received with downcast eyes, slumped shoulders, and a sigh, then your words have been too harsh. Abandonment rather than improvement will occur. If words are motivational, then the young one will most likely tackle the problem again.

My fourth child had difficulty learning to tie her shoes. When her shoes would become untied at preschool, her teacher would scold her and say, "You need to practice tying your shoes."

Frankly, I didn't see the need. No reason to get worked up. (Remember, this was my *fourth* kid.) I knew in time she'd be able to tie her shoes successfully and I told her so. Shaming wasn't the answer. So rather than send her to preschool in shoes with strings, she wore Velcro shoes.

On her first day of kindergarten she wanted to wear her fancy tie shoes. She still had not mastered the skill of making those bows. She donned her new shoes, and I secured the laces nice and tight, even adding double knots just in case. At the end of the day I went to pick her up. She was bursting with excitement, her eyes sparkling with joy.

"Mommy, I asked Mr. Brown if he could tie my shoes when they got loose. You know what he said? 'I'd be glad to!'"

After that loving exchange with the teacher and the knowledge that someday she'd be able to accomplish the task, she suddenly had a big desire to learn how to tie her shoes. No pressure, just lots of love.

Bɪᴛ ʙʏ Bɪᴛ

Disabilities like Attention Deficit Disorder or Attention Deficit Hyperactivity Disorder (ADD or ADHD) affect the ability to learn and to be still. But that doesn't mean patience can't increase and learning is impossible; it's just a little more challenging. Becky and I tell parents to break down the time periods for being in one place or concentrating on one topic. Then slowly stretch out the time. Measure the child's success by documenting it on a graph. Then celebrate as the attention span increases. The length of time it takes to improve will vary according to child and task. Don't make the mistake of assuming your child is unable to focus or sit still. Work on developing those abilities as you would any skill to be learned. Talk with your child's teacher and pediatrician to determine the best way to meet your youngster's needs. In some cases medical intervention is part of the solution.

Work Ethic

As a culture we have gone overboard with false hope and insincere encouragement. Just because our child dreams it doesn't make it so. For dreams to become reality, hard work is usually part of the puzzle.

Mike Freitag, executive director of coaching at Colorado Youth Soccer, says, "Complacency and entitlement have replaced competition. The end result is that players struggle to achieve when resistance increases… Instead of staying and working harder, or playing better, or playing the way the coach wants, it's just too easy to leave. Problems develop when we set goals for our kids without carefully taking into account the reality of the child's nature."[30]

The parent provides the framework and filter by which the child views life. Training a young one to try his hardest and to do his best will help him realize his dreams and passions. Have the elementary child learn to set his own goals. Give loving and honest feedback. Support the child as he works to attain his goal. This will counter the culture of complacency and entitlement.

A True Assessment

Hard work is one part of success in sports. Natural talent is another component. Even with a tenacious spirit, some things aren't meant to be.

The summer following kindergarten my (Becky) son wanted to play soccer. He loved to run and he was fast! I signed him up. He had high hopes, thinking his speed would make him a good player. He chased the ball in the huddle, often getting bruised. As goalie, he got his foot tangled in the net and the other team scored. Each week he was caked in mud, running through the rain-soaked fields. He hated it. He begged not to go to practice. Because he was part of the team, he had to go. My husband worked with him in the back yard, practicing passing and shooting. In the last game, he scored! He ended his career on a high note. Scott and I did not encourage him to continue. It wasn't his best sport! That's okay. He has other talents. Fast wheels on a hard worker don't guarantee a skillful soccer player. You have to know when to cut your losses.

The end of the season is a natural time to conclude participation in a sport. Dropping during the middle of a season can put the team in a bad position. Commitment is a part of tenacity. When children choose to participate in an activity, it is important to see it through to the end, to finish what was started. Unless the child is injured or there is some extenuating circumstance, following through on an obligation is good practice. Encourage and support the child in his perseverance. When a child learns commitment, he is less likely to be a quitter.

TMI

Too Much Information. Some parents burden their children with too much information. They inform the child of what the "experts" say he can or cannot do according to his specific challenge. Special education teacher Lori Hayda Felton advises this strategy:

> Don't discuss your child's challenges within earshot of the child. The child will not try if he thinks there is no point in exerting any effort. He may begin to say, "I can't _____ because of my disability." He will give up and make an excuse before even trying. Without realizing it the parents have enabled their child to become more dependent on others. It's possible certain accommodations must be made but it is also important to allow the child to feel some discomfort when learning a new skill.[31]

Felton goes on to recommend finding success in little things. It may be as small as the physically handicapped youngster getting himself a glass of water.

Many parents of a severely or profoundly handicapped child do everything for that child because they feel a sense of guilt over their young one's condition. The child is never given a chance to struggle. Although hard to watch, some struggle is necessary in the learning process.

Felton encourages parents to be lovingly firm. Parents need to rejoice in the smaller victories and goals even when the child fails at other things. Teach life skills. Understand for some mentally handicapped kids their social skills may not be typical. Try not to be overly concerned with some of the atypical social behaviors exhibited by mentally challenged individuals.

My (Lori) daughter and her friend helped out at a basketball clinic supported by The Sports Center for the Disabled and the Denver Nuggets basketball team. The volunteers, made up of professional basketball players and teenagers, assisted the mentally challenged kids on the court. Every time one little boy got the ball and made a play, he would lie down on the court and strike a pose. Other kids attending the clinic insisted on calling one of the Nuggets players by a better-known player's name, even after the players had been introduced. Of course, socially none of this was the norm, but these kids break the mold. Leave room to accept the exceptional.

Good Grief

Our kids will have difficulty, disappointment, and loss in life. Between the Wildenberg and Danielson families, our children have experienced the death of grandparents, friends, and pets. Grief is heavy.

When your child experiences loss, anger could be the dominant emotion expressed, especially if your child is nine years old or older. He may even be angry with God. Rather than focusing on the anger, help him through the emotions, allowing the angry outburst. Let the anger be his not yours. Your child needs a safe place to express his feelings. Do not be defensive if the emotion is directed at you. It isn't about you; it is about the pain.

At some point, in His perfect timing, God redeems suffering and moves us toward compassion. We are so thankful we have a sympathetic high priest who understands our heartaches and pain.

The shortest verse in the Bible is this: "Jesus wept" (John 11:35). It's short yet packed with meaning. Jesus knows what it is like to experience loss. In His humanness He experienced death and grief. The Lord is patient with us in our times of sorrow. Jesus grieved for His friend Lazarus, King David grieved the loss of his baby, Isaac grieved his mother's death, and Jacob grieved for his son Joseph.

God is big enough to take our anger and our doubts. The Bible even records honest questions and angry prayers (Job, David, and Jeremiah). When a child is angry due to suffering, it is important for parents to remain calm, listening empathetically. In the midst of hardship, try to keep your behavioral expectations as consistent as possible. Allow opportunities for your youngster to express his feelings, leaving room for expressions of anger or frustration. Acknowledge those feelings. If the issue is a death, even a pet goldfish, let him say goodbye. Planning and carrying out a funeral service for the pet is healing. Use real language not euphemisms. The fish isn't sleeping, it is dead. Don't be afraid of using words like *death* or *dying*. We don't want to confuse the young child or make him afraid of sleeping or getting sick. Make a distinction between sick and deathly ill. Don't say, "He got sick, so he died."

Provide some flexibility in the schedule to meet the child's needs. Continue to enforce limits, keep respect for family members intact, and provide some reasonable options for the child. Introduce the concept of heaven when discussing death with your child.

> **WHEN YOUR CHILD EXPERIENCES LOSS, ANGER COULD BE THE DOMINANT EMOTION EXPRESSED.**

GET REAL

None of us are immune to suffering. It comes to the innocent and guilty alike, zero discrimination. I (Lori but I'd really prefer to put Becky's name here!) came to understand this a few years ago.

It was the final day of a Bible study when the participants had an opportunity to share how God moved in their lives. I watched as a woman in her early forties walked with perfect posture to the front of the sanctuary, not a hair out of place. She was wearing a perky red dress with stilettos to match. I sinisterly thought, *Maybe she's going to describe how she dealt with a hangnail.*

As this beautiful woman spoke, I learned just how wrong my thoughts had been. She told a tragic story. Her stepson had died in the back yard while playing on the swing set. Her older teenaged stepson has struggled ever since. She poured out her heart. I was ashamed of mine. She looked as if she had it all together, so I assumed she'd never struggled. God knew the courage she needed to speak, the vulnerability to say she knew God was sovereign. God looks at the heart (1 Samuel 16:7). What He saw in mine that day wasn't pretty.

This serves as a reminder that every family deals with something. From the outside, other families may look like they have it all together. Jealousy stirs. But no family is perfect. Each has its own set of troubles.

Take It Away

When we suffer, we want to make the pain go away, now. Ask and God will answer. "He does not ignore the cries of the afflicted" (Psalm 9:12b). God's answer will be "Yes," "No," or "Wait." When praying for suffering to be removed, pray for God's will and be ready to surrender to whatever His answer will be. That's what Jesus did in the Garden of Gethsemane, praying, "Father, if you are willing, take this cup from me; yet not my will, but yours be done" (Luke 22:42).

My (Lori) daughter received a phone call late one Easter night. Her friend had called to say her eight-year-old brother was in the hospital with a life-threatening tumor. My daughter and I immediately went to the hospital. We joined our friends, their family, and others at the hospital. We prayed in the waiting room. Petitions of healing were spoken. Tears were shed.

Then the mother of the ill boy spoke to God. "Lord, I trust You. You love him more than I do."

What incredible faith! She knew where to place her hope. Five years later her son is cancer free. God is using this family in a mighty way to be His witness to other families struggling with terminal illness. "Praise be to the God and Father of our Lord Jesus Christ, the Father of compassion and the God of all comfort, who comforts us in all our troubles, so that we can comfort those in any trouble with the comfort we ourselves receive from God" (2 Corinthians 1:3-4). God never wastes suffering. Suffering can be the catalyst in us demonstrating God's glory. Trust God and remember that suffering always precedes glory and there is always a purpose in the pain.

> ## SUFFERING CAN BE THE CATALYST IN US DEMONSTRATING GOD'S GLORY.

BREAKING FREE

Suffering can happen in a child's peer relationships. Not being invited to a birthday party is hurtful. A sibling may not stick up for another during a critical moment, allegiances in friendships may shift, and parents may divorce. All are painful experiences. Jesus understands betrayal. Our children will not escape betrayal either.

No child, no adult, likes the feeling of being excluded. One little girl was repeatedly left out. She felt hurt and betrayed each time her two best friends would be together and she was not included. Her mother attempted to speak with both girls' parents, hoping to stir some sympathetic support but to no avail.

This mom hurt for her child. She and I (Becky) brainstormed ways of healing her daughter's heart and breaking out of the hurtful relationship. The mom decided to remind her daughter how deeply God and her family loved her. Then she encouraged her child to work on expanding her friendship base, focusing on making new friends and participating in activities apart from the two girls.

In this case, betrayal promoted a healthy change. God used this difficult situation to the good. The little girl now has a number of new pals at swimming and dance lessons, church, and school.

In cases where your child has been betrayed, provide time to be together and talk. Allow your child to vent. Be the Consultant and ask him how he would like to handle the situation. Be the Coach and be supportive. As the Chum, show empathy and share a time you were hurt.

Find something to laugh about. Make a plan for how to proceed. Decide if a conversation should take place between the betrayer and betrayed. If the betrayal has occurred in the family, then have your kids work it out and be there to guide. Family members need to remain loyal and demonstrate trustworthiness. Teach children of all ages about confidentiality and how to keep a confidence. Talk with your child to come up with a plan on how to forgive. Home needs to be a place of security.

WHAT'S THE POINT?

Why pray to a sovereign God who knows everything, including the outcome? Paul wrote in Romans 12:12, "Be joyful in hope, patient in affliction, faithful in prayer." Everyone experiences times when we cannot pray, times filled with exhaustion or heartache. When this happens, we can rely on other believers and trust the Holy Spirit to pray on our behalf. "In the same way, the Spirit helps us in our weakness. We do not know what we ought to pray for, but the Spirit himself intercedes for us" (Romans 8:26). If children are in a place where they cannot pray, then don't force the issue. Along with the Holy Spirit, pray for them instead.

God wants to hear about big and small struggles. In the summer before my (Lori) son started kindergarten he developed a wart on his finger, making handwriting difficult. All attempts to get rid of it failed. My son and I prayed for the wart to leave. Just before school began he noticed his wart was gone. God heard, God healed, and a boy's young faith increased. So what is the point of prayer? Prayer matters to God. If Jesus prayed, then so should we.

> **IF CHILDREN ARE IN A PLACE WHERE THEY CANNOT PRAY, THEN DON'T FORCE THE ISSUE. PRAY FOR THEM INSTEAD.**

DEEPER AND SWEETER

The following profound passage about love is found in the book *One Inch from the Fence* by Wes Seeliger:

The intensive care waiting room is different from any other place in the world. And the people who wait are different. They can't do enough for each other. No one is rude. The distinctions of race and class melt away. A person is a father first, a black man second. The garbage man loves his wife as much as the university professor loves his, and everyone understands this. Each person pulls for everyone else. In the intensive care waiting room, the world changes. Vanity and pretense vanish. The universe is focused on the doctor's next report. If only it will show improvement. Everyone knows that loving someone else is what life is all about.[32]

A possible purpose of suffering could be learning to love like the love seen in the ICU, deeper and sweeter. Compassion is learned in suffering. Resiliency and determination are the direct results of hope and perseverance in the midst of trials. With honest affirmation, support and nurture your child during the difficult times in his life. In adversity, he will grow in confidence, tenderness, and faith.

LOVE NOTES ON TENACITY

LORI WRITES: Being a mom has taught me a lot about what it means to *hang in there*. It has also helped me determine what is worth the fight and what isn't. Some things just aren't that important and adversity is not a bad word. Faith and character development are the most important elements in parenting.

BECKY WRITES: I think tenacity is built into a mom's DNA. When life gets tough for my kids, I feel my tenacity meter rise. I am my kids' cheerleader, encouraging them to persevere. When life pulls them down, with God's help, I give them a boost.

QUESTIONS

1. What struggles is your child experiencing? How can you support him?

2. In what area of your child's life can you encourage him to be tenacious and persevere?

3. Where have you seen God's loving compassion during your suffering or your child's?

PARENTING TIPS

1. Provide a stable environment with a flexible schedule when your child is grieving.

2. Pray with your child regarding small and big struggles.

3. Encourage family loyalty and confidentiality.

PRAYER

Father,

Thank You for Your tenacious love. Allow me to love as You love. Give me strength to persevere through the challenges life presents. Assist me in correcting my children with love rather than with criticism. My children learn in many different ways. Aid me in determining the best learning style for each one. Help me to be a respectful advocate for my children. In loss, give my family Your loving compassion to ease the pain of our grief. Let me be tenacious for Your glory.

In Your holy name I pray,

Amen

BLESSED IS THE MAN WHO PERSEVERES UNDER TRIAL
BECAUSE, WHEN HE HAS STOOD THE TEST,
HE WILL RECEIVE THE CROWN OF LIFE
THAT GOD HAS PROMISED TO THOSE WHO LOVE HIM.

James 1:12

SECTION EIGHT

LOVE IS ULTIMATE STRENGTH

CHOOSE TO FLOURISH

CONCLUSION

CHOOSE TO FLOURISH

LOVE NEVER FAILS.

1 Corinthians 13:8

BLOSSOMING

The first day of kindergarten for my (Lori) youngest was long-awaited. She yearned to carry a backpack and get on the big yellow bus just like her sisters and brother, to be a big kid. Tom and I waited at the stop along with our four children and the neighborhood kids. Excitement was in the air for the kids. I felt a heaviness. It was the end of an era. (Some parents feel elated at this milestone, but not me.)

The bus pulled up. My littlest fell into line with the others. The whole gang got on the bus, the doors shut, and off they went. I waved. No return wave.

"She didn't even look back," I said. My heart hurt a little. Okay, my heart hurt a lot.

"Isn't that what we want," my husband said, "for her to be excited about school? It's only a couple of hours."

Tom's reasoning did not alter my emotions. My vision blurred, my cheeks dampened.

Growth happens right before our eyes. First words, first steps, first day of school. Momentous occasions. Growth that flourishes has been nurtured by love.

A Different Drummer

Our children may not be the people we expected them to be. They will grow in their own way. Kids can do some strange things. Parents may be taken off guard with the unusual, quirky stuff. My (Lori) preschool son wore buckets on his head for over a year. He went from one bucket to a stack in a matter of a few months. He wore his buckets everywhere!

Letting kids be who they are, not squelching the atypical behavior, helps them feel accepted. Being creative and working with your child's uniqueness is smart parenting.

One mom said she couldn't give her child the daily job of setting the table because it would turn into a fiasco. "She'll get distracted and start to create a centerpiece for the table rather than put out the plates and silverware."

This woman's daughter is gifted with an artistic flair but lacks focus. She needed an appropriate outlet for her creativity within certain boundaries. Now when her child is given the job of setting the table, first the basic task must be completed. Then the little girl can decorate to her heart's content until dinnertime. By actually embracing and working with a little oddity in the home, the child feels valued and understood.

The Scale

As toddlers grow to preschoolers and preschoolers to elementary students, parenting styles will change. Specific direction is needed for the toddler to navigate his day. The elementary-aged child needs room to make some choices. The preschooler needs a mixture of both experiences. The most intense parenting is with the toddler. By slowly backing off as the child ages and gains experience, the parents will grant the child the opportunity to experience success and failure. Be involved but don't take over. Let him grow.

Parenting is fluid. Be prepared to jump from Chum to Controller at any given moment. Use a mixture of the four desirable techniques: Controller, Chum, Coach, and Consultant. Avoid camping on one type too long. Balance the relational and rules approaches.

Breathe In

God breathed His breath of life into each of us (Genesis 2:7). The acronym B.R.E.A.T.H. helps us to remember six ways to approach raising kids:

B.R.E.A.T.H.

B = Bent - know and study your child

R = Rejoice in his successes

E = Express empathy for the challenges

A = Avoid comparisons with siblings

T = Talents are appreciated

H = Has Purpose

Our kids need to hold onto the belief that they're worthy and valuable because God created them and breathed life into them. Love, acceptance, and forgiveness are ties that bind family members to each other. These loving qualities will empower children to discover God's purpose for them. They will feel more confident to step out, believing they are worthy, valuable, and capable.

The Soil

We have presented fourteen elements (using the chapter titles of this book) that make great soil for raising little kids. Living these virtues will make the fifteenth characteristic of flourishing love possible. Reading God's Word, praying, examining circumstances, and getting wise counsel from other believers are all critical to parenting your best. Unfortunately, the verse "Train a child in the way he should go, and when he is old he will not turn from it" (Proverbs 22:6) isn't a promise but it is a wise saying, an observation. Here are some basic principles to live by in your home as you train up a child well:

- ♥ Love God.
- ♥ Love others as you love yourself.
- ♥ Do onto others as you would have them do onto you.
- ♥ Forgive as you have been forgiven.
- ♥ Have an attitude of gratitude.

Of course this side of heaven we will not love perfectly. Every parent who picks up a parenting book has a reason for choosing it. Whatever your reason for reading *The 1 Corinthians 13 Parent: Raising Little Kids with Big Love*, we hope you felt encouraged and motivated rather than overwhelmed, discouraged, or shamed. Our goal is to help parents of young kids realize that parenting is more than gaining cooperation and getting appropriate behavior. We want our children to be motivated to do things in the right way with the right heart. That isn't to say obedience isn't important. Of course it is. A child behaving as expected, even when not really wanting to, shows respect and self-control. The child's outward actions are a reflection of his inward spirit. When the heart is right, the behavior follows. A good parent trains for both short-term obedience and long-term character development.

The qualities of imperfection and the experience of suffering are ways God draws us and our kids to Himself. In 1 Corinthians 13 He shows us the most excellent way to love and raise children. Demonstrating patience increases a child's self-worth. Kindness in word and deed cements family unity. A child who lives in a home where contentment, humility, respect, and unselfishness reign, values people over personal gain. Choosing to show self-control in volatile moments is loving and constructive. Having a home that is permeated with a forgiving spirit takes the sting out of making mistakes.

Children have an easier time choosing right over wrong when they are brought up in a home that embraces absolute truth. Protecting and trusting are ways to live out love. Hope and the desire to persevere are the final qualities that demonstrate growth. Our kids will flourish when they are raised with the type of love described in 1 Corinthians 13. We will never parent perfectly and our children will never be perfect. But the more we are like Jesus, the more we'll be able to love as He loves us.

Sow What?

Pastor John Crosby challenges his congregation, "Allow your faith to outlive you."[33] Our legacy of faith is the most valuable gift our children can inherit. But they need to claim it as their own before they can receive the inheritance. Our biggest job is to plant the seeds of faith in our children. We pray those seeds will take strong root, blossom, and spread.

We want to encourage you in this process. No one is better suited to impact your kids each day than you! Introduce young children to Jesus. Talk about what Jesus has done for us all. Read God's Word and use it to teach right and wrong. Use the ABCs when leading little ones to Jesus.

A - ASK JESUS TO FORGIVE YOUR SINS.
B - BELIEVE IN YOUR HEART GOD RAISED JESUS FROM THE DEAD.
C - CONFESS WITH YOUR MOUTH JESUS IS LORD.

"If you confess with your mouth, 'Jesus is Lord,' and believe in your heart that God raised him from the dead, you will be saved. For it is with your heart that you believe and are justified, and it is with your mouth that you confess and are saved" (Romans 10:9-10). Jesus Christ is the legacy of love God graciously gives.

CONCLUDING PRAYER

Heavenly Father,
Thank You for the gifts of Your Son, Your Word, and Your Spirit. Thank You that You demonstrate, illustrate, and illuminate the most excellent way to raise children. Forgive my parenting failures. Use them to teach me and to draw me closer to You. Bless my family with Your abundant love. Give each of us a tender heart for each other. I pray we all may have a heart that recklessly seeks after You, our eternal Father.
Amen

FAITH, HOPE AND LOVE. BUT THE GREATEST OF THESE IS LOVE.

1 Corinthians 13:13b-c

Love is...

Patient, kind, content, humble, respectful, unselfish, peaceful, forgiving, and good.

It communicates truth, protection, trust, and hope.

Love is tenacious.

It is the catalyst to flourishing growth.

Love is...GOD.

Post Script......Love Is a Journey

P.S. From Lori and Becky,

We intimately know your desire to raise your children the best way you can while honoring God. We feel your agony during the struggles and your elation in the victories. We pray that you and your family will be blessed by the powerful, life-giving words in 1 Corinthians 13. If you want to connect with us, you can reach Lori at www.loriwildenberg.com or Becky at www.beckydanielson.com.

In His love,

L & B

Bread of Heaven

So now we start but without merit

Father please show us your way

Grant us Your grace that we inherit

Christ our bread today

Amen

-Rockman[34]

Follow the way of love.

1 Corinthians 14:1a

Appendix

A–Zs of Cooperative Interaction

Accept uniqueness, parent and child's uniqueness. Let each parent establish a personal relationship with the child. What works with one child may not work with another; what works one day may not work the next.

Beat the clock. For a dawdler, make the timer the bad guy. Set the timer. It rings, the child's task must be done.

Clear, concise instructions that are short, sweet, and positive. Say what to do versus what not to do. For example, "Sit down," rather than, "Don't stand."

Distraction is good for toddlers and early preschool-age children. Use distractions for safety issues or when diffusing frustration or anger.

Expectations. Remember age, stage, and temperament of the child. Don't expect too much or too little. Limits are flexible: Children want more and parents want less.

Forgive and forget. Forgive self for discipline mistakes. Think of other ways to handle a situation. Forgive child for misbehavior then use positive prevention. For example, tell what behavior is wanted and expected before an upcoming activity. Don't be a historian, reminding the child of a previous bad situation.

Give a warning before a transition. For example, "Turn off the DVD in five minutes," or "Do your favorite thing before we leave the park."

Humor can be an attention-getter, a tantrum-diffuser, or mood-changer but use cautiously without sarcasm.

If this, then that. "*If* you hit your sister on the head with the bat, *then* I will take it away." Remove item for part of the day, for example, until breakfast, lunch, or dinner. Put item on top of fridge so they can see it. Let the child know it will be returned before the next part of the day. But then the toy must be used as intended.

Jump in! When it's time to clean up, join the kids. If you don't jump in, then they won't think you mean what you are saying. As kids get older, give them a specific job. Don't redo what they have done. They need pride in completion and accomplishment.

Keep cool! Tantrums and attitudes that are not yours, so don't take them on. Remove yourself mentally for a minute to regain control. Use a rage interrupter, such as repeating, "Love is patient and kind."

Lots of love. Say, "I love you." "I will never leave you." "I will help you move faster." Say a quick, "1, 2, 3," and then act on your word.

Mean it! When you say whatever, mean it and move on it. Say it and expect cooperation. For example, if a directive to come is ignored by the child, then go and get him.

No means no and yes means yes. Use the phrase "I need to think about it" to give yourself decision-making time. Be true to your word to build security and trust.

Offer choices, but only two acceptable choices that you and the child can live with. Use sparingly, since having too many decisions is confusing. Remember, the child doesn't always have a choice.

Positive prevention is best to avoid a potentially stressful situation. Before walking into a store tell the child, "Keep your hands to yourself."

Quiet voice, the great attention-getter: Whisper in ear, touch child, and get close. The quieter the voice and the closer the speaker, the greater the message.

Regular routine during the week. Be flexible on weekends.

State the problem in a question form: "Uh oh! The toys are on the floor and we want to play outside. What should we do?"

Trade for a time. Learning to share can be taught by trading toys and timing the sharing. Other ways to encourage sharing include having one child cut the treat and letting the other have first pick, and allowing the guest to choose toys and activities first. Remember, don't share the most special toy. Put it away when a guest comes to visit.

Unity as a couple. Be on the same page with your spouse regarding rules and consequences for broken rules.

Very consistent in the family rules. The rules are the same at home as when away from home.

Write the rules as a family. Five rules or less, posted, stated in positive way: (1) Respect God; (2) Respect others; (3) Respect self; (4) Respect things; etc.

Xamine the circumstances to assess the situation. For example, if the child has not napped, then maybe it's not the best time to run errands. If you choose to go, then be ready for the ramifications of your choice.

Yes, after. For example, if child says, "May I go to my friend's house?" then the parent replies, "Yes, after…you pick up your toys."

Zip it! Pick your battles. Let some kid stuff go. For example, allow her to wear the princess dress to church.

NOTES

CHAPTER THREE

1. Joanne Miller, RN, BSN, "Everyday Parents Can Raise Extraordinary Kids!" (lecture, L.I.F.E. Fellowship Fredrick Campus, Fredrick, CO, September 25, 2010). Joanne Miller is the co-founder of the National Center for Biblical Parenting. She is the coauthor of *Parenting is Heart Work* (2005) and *Say Goodbye to Whining, Complaining and Bad Attitudes* (2000). Her desire to encourage a friendship between her children is a model for parents.

CHAPTER SIX

2. William J. Doherty and Barbara Z. Carlson, *Putting Family First: Successful Strategies for Reclaiming Family Life in a Hurry-up World* (New York: Henry Holt, 2002), 32. Dr. Doherty, professor at the University of Minnesota's Department of Family Social Science, author, and speaker, and Mrs. Carlson, author and speaker, cofounded the organization Putting Family First. The book provides research substantiating the benefits of family dinners and gives suggestions for implementing the practice of family dinnertime.

3. Kathy Namura, e-mail message to author, June 01, 2010. Kathy Namura is a veteran principal. She reveals the effects stress can have on children when expectations are unrealistic.

4. Keri Buisman, MAED, e-mail message to author, June 02, 2010. Keri Buisman is an adjunct professor at St. Mary's University, Minneapolis, MN. She shares the story of her daughter's selfless giving.

5. Pastor Larry Renoe, "Elders" (sermon, WaterStone Community Church, Littleton, CO, June 06, 2010). Larry Renoe is the teaching pastor at Waterstone Community Church. The condition of a servant's heart is noted.

CHAPTER SEVEN

6. Dr. Scott Turansky, "Everyday Parents Can Raise ExtraordinaryKids!" (lecture, L.I.F.E. Fellowship Fredrick Campus, Fredrick, CO, September 25, 2010). Dr. Turansky is the co-founder of the National Center for Biblical Parenting and coauthor of *Parenting Is Heart Work* (2005) and *Say Goodbye to Whining, Complaining and Bad Attitudes* (2000). He addresses the effects of anger in the family.

7. Ibid.

CHAPTER EIGHT

8. Mary Heathman, "The Purpose of Attraction" (lecture, Where Grace Abounds, Denver, CO, June 24, 2010). Mary Heathman is the founder of Where Grace Abounds. Her ministry assists with sexual and relational conflicts. An illustration of broken trust and the need for confession is used.

9. Robin Chaddock, "Soul Snacks," accessed June 02, 2010, http://www.robinchaddock.com. Robin Chaddock shares her thoughts on forgiveness on her blog Soul Snacks. (Site discontinued.)

10. *The Power of a Praying® Parent*, copyright 1995/2005 by Stormie Omartian, Eugene, Oregon 97402, www.harvest house publishers.com. Used by permission. Her wise words encourage family members to forgive through the power of prayer.

CHAPTER NINE

11. Taken from *The Strong Family* by Charles R. Swindol. Copyright © 1991 by Zondervan. Used by permission of Zondervan. www.zondervan.com. Charles Swindoll offers parents advice in dealing with evil in a child's life.

12. Taken from *Respectable Sins: Confronting the Sins We Tolerate* by Jerry Bridges. Copyright ©2007 by Tyndale House Publishers, Inc. All rights reserved. The author notes the power and guidance of the Holy Spirit is available for Christians.

13. John Maxwell as quoted in Dave Jacobs, *Resources and Encouragement for Pastors and Church Leaders,* "You Teach What You Know but Reproduce What You Are," July 04, 2011, accessed September 04, 2011, from http://davejacobs.net.

14. Charles H. Spurgeon, *Promises and Prayers for Women* (Grand Rapids: Family Christian Press, 2007), 51. "Of two evils, choose neither."

CHAPTER TEN

15. Betty Shannon Cloyd, *Children and Prayer: A Shared Pilgrimage* (Nashville: Upper Room Books, 1997), 31. The author encourages parents to live out their faith for their children to witness.

16. Taken from *Heaven for Kids* by Randy C. Alcorn and Linda M. Washington. Copyright ©2006 by Tyndale House Publishers, Inc. Used by permission of Tyndale House Publishers, Inc. All rights reserved. Randy C. Alcorn describes heaven in terms children can understand.

17. Lori Wildenberg and Becky Danielson, *Empowered Parents: Putting Faith First* (Gainesville: Synergy, 2003), 135. Eternal moments are defined.

18. C. S. Lewis, *Mere Christianity* (New York: HarperOne, 1980), 225. C. S. Lewis poignantly states how we can become more like our Lord.

19. Dale Salwak, *Faith in the Family: Honoring and Strengthening Home and Spirit* (Novato: New World Library, 2001), 197. Trust is described as a binding force in family life.

CHAPTER ELEVEN

20. Hector Cantu and Carlos Castellanos, "Baldo," *Denver Post* September 03, 2011. The comic identifies the extreme in safety concerns.

21. Hara Estroff Marano, "A Nation of Wimps," *Psychology Today*, November 01, 2004, http://www.psychologytoday.com/print/21819. Children learn life skills through having to deal with difficulties rather than being sheltered from them.

22. Kathy Namura, e-mail message to author, June 01, 2010. Strategies for working with teachers in the best interests of the child are offered for parents.

CHAPTER TWELVE

23. Cecil Murphey, *Invading the Privacy of God: Rush into God's Presence, Revitalize Your Prayer Life, Put an End to Devotional Boredom* (Ann Arbor: Vine, 1997), 140. The author suggests the reason we feel the need to lie.

CHAPTER THIRTEEN

24. Kathy Namura, e-mail message to author, June 01, 2010. The veteran principal shares her perspective on how parents can successfully work with teachers to provide a positive learning experience for the special needs child.

25. Dr. H. Norman Wright, *Experiencing Grief* (Nashville: Broadman and Holman, 2004), 53. Belief statements of people who are resilient are shared.

26. *The New Guide to Crisis and Trauma Counseling: A practical Guide for Ministers, Counselors, and Lay Counselors* by Dr. H. Norman Wright, p. 350. Copyright ©2003 Light/Regal Books, Ventura, CA 93003. Used by permission. The seven signs of depression found in children are described.

27. Ibid. *The New Guide to Crisis and Trauma Counseling: A practical Guide for Ministers, Counselors, and Lay Counselors* by Dr. H. Norman Wright, p. 350.

Copyright ©2003 Light/Regal Books, Ventura, CA 93003. Dr. H. Norman Wright identifies the causes of depression in children.

28. Ibid., 350-351. Suggestions for parents about how to assist children dealing with depression are provided.

29. Taken from *My Utmost for His Highest* by Oswald Chambers, © 1935 by Dodd Mead & Co., renewed © 1963 by the Oswald Chambers Publications Assn., Ltd. Used by permission of Discovery House Publishers, Box 3566, Grand Rapids, MI 49501. All rights reserved. We are reminded that hope waits upon God in times of disappointment.

CHAPTER FOURTEEN

30. Mike Freitag, "Fun or Fear: What Motivates Young Players?" *Goal Post Scripts,* September 05, 2011, 10. The author notes the effects of complacency and entitlement on children in competitive sports.

31. Lori Hayda Felton (Special education teacher, ISD 624, White Bear Lake, MN). Telephone interview with author, September 08, 2011. The special education instructor shares her observations on kids with special needs.

32. Wes Seeliger, *One Inch from the Fence* (Atlanta: Forum House, 1973), 10. A model for compassionate love is seen in the ICU.

CONCLUSION

33. Pastor John Crosby, "Faith that Moves" (sermon, Christ Presbyterian Church, Edina, MN, September 18, 2011). This senior pastor at Christ Presbyterian Church in Edina, Minnesota, encourages all Christians to share the gospel, allowing faith to grow in others.

34. Rockman is the pen name for Dr. Robert Appel, the author of the poem *Bread of Heaven.* Edina, MN. Rockman is Lori's dad. His poetry is a loving tribute to Jesus, his Lord and Savior.

Index

About the Authors

Lori Wildenberg

Lori Wildenberg knows full well the struggles a parent with little kids experiences. At one point, Lori had four kids, ages five and under! Lori is passionate about coming alongside parents to encourage, empower, strengthen, and support them. She communicates effectively with transparency, warmth, and gentle humor. Her straight-forward, realistic approach engages her audience and assists moms and dads in their quest to parent well. Lori has more than twenty-five years' experience working with parents and kids in both secular and faith-based settings. She is a licensed parent and family educator who meets parents where they are and helps them get to where they want to go. Lori openly shares her personal and professional experience using a "been there, done that" approach. Her parenting philosophy is focused on developing a child's heart and character; this sets her apart from many other parenting voices out there. Lori and her ministry partner, Becky Danielson, are founders of 1 Corinthians 13 Parenting. Together they have authored three faith-based parenting books, including the second 1 Corinthians 13 Parent book, Raising Big Kids with Supernatural Love. Lori is also a mentor mom with The M.O.M. Initiative and writes curriculum for and trains teachers at the Professional Learning Board.

The Wildenbergs live in the foothills of the Rocky Mountains. A perfect day in Lori's world is hiking with her husband, Tom, four kids, and labradoodle.

Lori is available for speaking, parent consulting, and teacher in-service training. Contact her at www.loriwildenberg.com or www.1Corinthians13Parenting.com.

BECKY DANIELSON, M.Ed.

Becky Danielson's favorite title is Mom. She and her husband, Scott, have two active and fun-loving teenage boys. She is a licensed Parent and Family educator and co-founder of 1 Corinthians 13 Parenting with her ministry partner, Lori Wildenberg. Above all she is a follower of Jesus Christ.

Becky has spent a lot of time in school as a learner, teacher, and volunteer. After attending Gustavus Adlophus College for her Bachelor's degree (K-6 Education, Early Childhood Education), she received her Master's degree from St. Mary's University, and a license in Parent and Family Education from Crown College. Before becoming a stay-at-home-mom, she taught kindergarten and first grade. The birth of her two boys changed her life and career completely. Sharing God's Word to equip and encourage families has become Becky's passion. The parents she works with, either in a large group setting or one-on-one mentoring, find her warm, honest, and supportive. Her ideas and parenting tips are practical, encouraging, and applicable. Becky candidly shares her life as a Christian wife, mom, and educator. Along with co-authoring the 1 Corinthians 13 Parent books, Becky contributes to Hooray for Family, a print and online magazine, The Pearl Girls, and Faith Village. When she's not writing or meeting with moms and dads, Becky can be found in her kitchen garden, reading, or on an adventure with her Danielson men!

Connect with Becky at www.beckydanielson.com or www.1Corinthians13Parenting.com.

READERS RESPONSES TO
RAISING LITTLE KIDS WITH BIG LOVE

Raising Little Kids with Big Love was useful and informative. We had many moments of "Oh, that's how you deal with that!" We look forward to referring to it over and over again.

-Ken and Kerry parents of 4 kids
ages 7, 5, 2 and 5 weeks,
Littleton, CO

Concise, thought provoking, helpful and transformative. I really like the questions, parenting tips, prayers and quotes. Loved all the personal illustrations and the Scripture in *Raising Little Kids with Big Love*.

-Melonie, mother of 2 (6 and 3),
Littleton, CO

A treasure of godly wisdom overflows from the pages of *Raising Little Kids with Big Love*. Lori and Becky provide delightful personal stories that highlight the positive and constructive ways to communicate truth and love to our children. If you desire practical and effective biblical ideas to help you understand your parenting style and build godly character in your children, *Raising Little Kids with Big Love*. is a must read.

-Nancy Ann Yaeger, mother of three,
author of *A Mother's Prayers for Her Children*
and *A Grandmother's Guide to Praying for Her Family*

Made in the USA
San Bernardino, CA
05 October 2014